GREAT GREENS

fresh, flavorful, and innovative recipes

BY GEORGEANNE BRENNAN   FOREWORD BY TODD KOONS
PHOTOGRAPHS BY FRANKIE FRANKENY

CHRONICLE BOOKS
SAN FRANCISCO

Library of Congress Cataloging-in-Publication Data available.

ISBN 0-8118-3991-5

This edition produced exclusively for Epic Roots, Inc.
by Chronicle Books LLC.

Manufactured in China.

Prop styling by Toby Hansen
Food styling by Diane Gsell
Designed by Design MW, New York

The photographer would like to thank Leslie Jonath for her
wise insight, Georganne Brennan for working on this project
and fabulous recipes, Diane and Toby for their consistently
great work, Lisa Campbell, Brett MacFadden, Abby Clawson
and Allison Muench Williams at Design MW, Wendy Mardigian,
Eli Mardigian-DesJardins, Eddy Gelsman, Cami Haecker and
a special thanks to Todd Koons at Epic Roots for allowing me to
produce this book.

10 9 8 7 6 5 4 3 2 1

Chronicle Books LLC
85 Second Street
San Francisco, California 94105

OPPOSITE PAGE: Romaine, Parsley, and Celery Salad with Shaved Parmesan (page 81).

acknowledgments

GEORGEANNE BRENNAN

First of all, I want to thank Todd Koons and Frankie Frankeny for inviting me to be part of this project. It has been a pleasure to work with them both. A special thanks to Melanie Bajakian, Ann Evans, and Ethel Brennan who helped make this book a reality in the kitchen, by cooking, testing, and tasting recipes with me. Thank you also to Diane Gsell and Toby Hansen who did such a wonderful job styling the recipes. I would also like to give a special thanks to my husband, Jim Schrupp, who is my favorite greens grower, to my longtime friend and former partner in Le Marchè Seeds, Charlotte Kimball, and to all the farmers I have known, large and small, from whom I have learned so much about growing greens.

At Chronicle Books I am especially appreciative of Lisa Campbell who kept this book on task. Thank you to Leslie Jonath, with whom I've worked on many books, for her editorial vision, and a heartfelt thanks to Erik Sandall, who did such a conscientious job of inputting. Thanks are also due to Carrie Bradley, for researching the nutritional information, and to Megan Flautt, for her valuable help.

TODD KOONS

The making of *Great Greens* happened with the support, encouragement, and hard work of several people whom I would like to thank.

Georgeanne Brennan undertook the creation of the manuscript and lent her skills both as author, cook, and an excellent grower of greens.

I am also grateful to Leslie Jonath, who guided our passion onto these pages.

My heartfelt thanks to my friend Lori T. Latta, whose keen sense of food and interest in all things green continues to inspire me.

Lastly, I appreciate the entire team at Epic Roots, particularly David Chelf who has worked closely with me from seed to salad with patience and humor, and to our photographer, Frankie Frankeny, whose efforts and faith in our work made all this possible.

57 soups CHAPTER 4

73 salads CHAPTER 5

97 main dishes CHAPTER 6

123 side dishes CHAPTER 7

138 index

143 table of equivalents

foreword by todd koons

I grew up around greens. Some of my fondest memories are from the days on my family farm near Eugene, Oregon, where I spent many hours during my childhood gardening with my grandmother, Lady Doris, and my mother, Karen. I was usually assigned the greens detail. Even back then, I loved to grow greens. It was my specialty. We lived the counterculture rural lifestyle of the '70s, which centered around a large vegetable garden and an open kitchen, where friends and family would gather for gourmet meals. This community included a number of individuals who deeply influenced the path I would later take.

A bright spot on that list of influential people is Georgeanne Brennan. I met her when she and her partner were giving a class on greens and lettuces in 1982, while I was cooking at Chez Panisse in Berkeley. I was already hooked on the baby greens that we were cultivating in local gardens and had been serving at the restaurant with much acclaim. Georgeanne obviously instructed me well, as I have spent the last twenty-five years of my life devoted to developing, growing, preparing, and serving greens. My connection with Georgeanne dates back to the days of my first farming venture, when she and her husband, Jim, provided many of the seeds from which we grew some of the nation's most popular greens.

Without her, I may never have experienced the tactile, sensual pleasure that comes from gently tossing a bowl of young lettuces and greens with my bare hands. Georgeanne introduced me to an entire world of unusual greens and encouraged me to experiment with them.

The versatility of greens is evident in their multitude of uses— whether they are balancing a main dish or standing alone. We are seeing a deeper interest in overall health and well-being, both in body and spirit. The powerful nutritional value of greens is nothing new, but as we evolve into a healthier society, we are embracing this knowledge and incorporating it into our lives. We are beginning to understand the positive impact of antioxidants, such as folic acid and lutein, as well as the long-standing bene-

fits of fiber and vitamins A and C—all of which are abundantly found in many greens.

This book celebrates greens and all their diversity. It begins with an overview and history of greens and includes the elements that go into making great greens—from a glossary of leaves to all the various items that transform greens into wonderfully healthful meals that will satisfy and inspire you to go after your own roots and connect with your food. Georgeanne's recipes are simple to prepare, quick to cook, varied, and original enough to keep bringing you back to the table of life—one dish you can't get enough of.

introduction

Great Greens celebrates the variety of ways that greens can be used in the kitchen. As you will discover, greens are amazingly versatile. In addition to their traditional role in salads, you can chop and sauté them, wrap them around fillings, stir them into soups, slow-cook them in flavorful liquid, and even deep-fry them. I love greens of every kind, so they make an appearance, in some fashion, on my table year-round. I incorporate them into quick and simple dishes, such as a creamy spinach gratin seasoned with nutmeg; pasta tossed with arugula, toasted walnuts, and lemon; or a salad of mâche topped with warm figs, hazelnuts, and goat cheese. I can't let a winter week go by without making sweet-and-sour red cabbage, or a summer night pass without some version of greens and sweet, ripe tomatoes.

Greens also play a role in my more elegant preparations, sometimes for company but just as often because I have a taste for them. Belgian endive, delicately braised in white wine and butter, or watercress soup makes a subtle accompaniment to roast chicken or poached fish. For a fancy brunch, I might prepare a chard and salmon tart, a composed salad with ahi tuna, watercress, and hard-boiled eggs, or perhaps risotto with escarole and lemon.

Not surprisingly, people have delighted in the flavors of greens since ancient times. All of the common greens we see in our produce departments and farmers' markets today have their origins in wild plants native to Europe, Africa, Asia, or the Americas. Our prehistoric ancestors gathered wild plants, such as the cabbage along the North Atlantic coast, the mâche of Europe and Africa, and the wide variety of wild spinaches found throughout Asia. By 6000 B.C., if not earlier, the wild plants were being domesticated.

Because of their flavor and the significant amounts of vitamins and minerals they provide, greens were a vital part of the diet of early man, just as they are of ours. We know that lettuce, which originated in the Near East, was grown and served to Persian kings before the time of Christ, and that brassicas, which include cabbage, were being cultivated in China by 6000 B.C. These early domesticated greens were most likely more primitive looking than their contemporary counterparts, but the collard plant, actually a type of kale, is still quite similar in appearance to the ancestral wild cabbage, with the same gray, rounded leaves.

Greens, both wild and cultivated, were as important on the ancient Greek and Roman table as they are today, and lettuce, chicories, and brassicas were all available then. In the second century B.C., as the Roman Empire expanded throughout the Mediterranean and trade increased with the East, so did the spread and cultivation of food plants, including greens. In the empire's lands, from Spain to Asia Minor, huge farms, called *latifundia,* were established, and their crops supplied the population with food. Many of these farms fell into disrepair and decline during the years following the fall of Rome.

However, by the time of Charlemagne in A.D. 812, when life in Europe had stabilized 400 years after the invasions, we find more than 200 species listed in his "Directions for the Administration of Imperial Courts or Estates." These include a number of our favorite contemporary greens—cabbage, endive, chicory, *roquette* (arugula), lettuce, and cress. During the next 1,200 years, humanity expanded its knowledge about plants. New ones were introduced into Europe and Asia from the New World, plants of European origins made their way east to Asia, and those of Asia traveled west.

Vilmorin-Andrieux, the oldest surviving seed company in the world, was established in France in the mid-1700s and was indicative of changes in Europe, where farmers, market growers, and gardeners were beginning to buy commercially produced seed rather than simply saving their own. Vilmorin's catalog of 1885 had a tremendous array of lettuces and greens, including several Asian greens. In much of Asia, however, individuals or groups continued to save their seeds, and large seed companies did not emerge until the twentieth century.

Greens are not new. What is new is the tremendous variety of fresh, flavorful greens currently available to us through our markets and the even greater selection of seeds available to farmers, market growers, and home gardeners. Today, seed catalogs feature an astonishing number of greens. Johnny's Selected Seeds, a popular source for both market growers and home gardeners, lists 53 varieties of lettuce alone. Under a separate category, "Greens," we find 33 different listings, over half of them Asian. At least one seed company, Reed's Seeds, is devoted entirely to cabbages.

I am proud and happy that I played a role in the proliferation and popularization of greens available today. In 1982, my partner, Charlotte Glenn, and I started Le Marché Seeds, a vegetable-seed import company. We were based in Northern California, but our catalog was mailed to home gardeners nationwide. Small farmers, many of them practicing organic methods, were starting up around the country, and they began requesting our catalog and asking for large quantities of seeds. These were the men and women who fueled the culinary revolution of the 1980s and 1990s. They were eager to try new vegetable and fruit varieties, just at a time when the American seed companies were phasing out many of their older varieties in favor of newer hybrids.

Charlotte and I traveled to France, Italy, England, Holland, and Mexico and met with the seed companies there. We explained that we were not interested in the new hybrids but in the older varieties, the kind listed in Vilmorin-Andrieux's catalog (which the English and French seedsmen all had close at hand on their office bookshelves). Once we told them we were interested in taste, above all, they became enthusiastic, sharing their favorite recipes, taking us to visit some of their farmers, telling us stories and histories about the varieties, and selling us seeds in quantities large enough to supply small farmers.

We wrote it all up in our annual catalog, complete with recipes. Our market-grower customers would call and ask if we had anything new or special, because they were now growing for a restaurant and the chef was looking for special lettuces and greens. We were the first company to import lettuces that are commonplace today, such as Lollo Rossa, Rouge d'Hiver, Cocarde, Merveille de Quatre Saisons, and Reine de Glace. We introduced Lacinato kale and French dandelion to the American marketplace as well as mesclun and a dozen different varieties of radicchio.

We closed Le Marché in 1991, after selling part of the company, and, by that time, the greens revolution was well under way. It is very gratifying to me today to see that mesclun mix, arugula, Rouge d'Hiver, and radicchio seeds are sold in chain home and garden stores, and that many of the once-exotic greens are now available fresh in supermarkets across the country, available to everyone.

I wrote *Great Greens* to inspire cooks to explore all the possibilities of greens, from iceberg and romaine lettuce to arugula and radicchio. Because I believe that information, not just recipes, is important, Chapter 1 gives an overview of greens, including availability, methods of growing, and cooking techniques. Chapter 2, designed as a one-stop resource, features a glossary that describes more than a dozen important greens and suggested uses of each, plus tips on shopping, storing, special preparation, gardening, and nutrition.

In the recipes, I suggest variations and substitutions whenever I can so that you easily create your own versions of these dishes year-round, based on your preferences and what is available at your local market. That is what I have done over the years, and I am constantly discovering new flavor combinations. I never tire of greens. Their infinite variety impresses me daily, and growing and cooking with them continues to give me and those around me great pleasure and satisfaction. I hope you will discover the pleasures of greens as well.

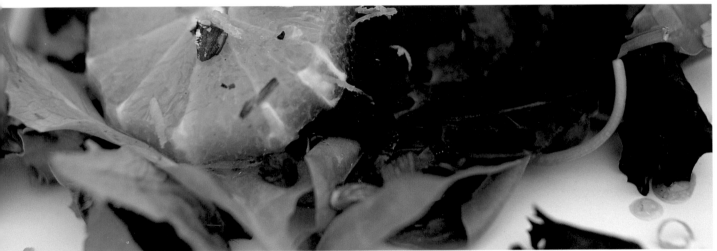

GREENS, AVAILABLE EVERY-
WHERE, ARE ASTONISHING IN
THEIR VERSATILITY, FLAVOR,
AND USES, AND CAN OFTEN
BE USED INTERCHANGEABLY
WITH ONE ANOTHER, WHICH
YOU'LL DISCOVER HERE.

As well as being ideal for salads, they can also be cooked in just about every way you can think of, from braising to stir-frying, even grilling and deep-frying. You'll find details on these cooking techniques in this chapter, plus suggestions for using cooked greens in a variety of ways, such as pizza toppings, pasta pairings, gratins, and side dishes with a twist.

OPPOSITE PAGE (*top to bottom*): Radicchio Rolls with Daikon Radish, Cucumber, Crab, and Avocado (page 46), Beet and Mesclun Salad with Blood Oranges and Goat Cheese (page 82), Creamed Spinach Gratin (page 124)

all about greens

The most popular European, Asian, and American greens, the ones that are the focus of this book, are available throughout the year. Traditionally, greens could be found in abundance during spring and fall, the time of year when cool weather engenders a plant's leafy growth. In summer's heat, when plants produce fruits and seeds, such as tomatoes and beans, or in the chilling cold of winter, when little grows, greens were often in short supply.

Today, due to the improvement of long-distance shipping, a wide range of high-quality greens can be found practically year-round in produce markets. Most of the year, many of them are grown in the cool temperate regions along California's coast and, in winter, in the warm regions of California, Texas, Arizona, and Florida.

If you shop at farmers' markets or produce stands, where the produce reflects local conditions, greens will be sparser in summer and winter than in spring and fall. There are some exceptions, however. Kale and radicchio are quite winter hardy and actually sweeten in below-freezing temperatures. Curly endive (frisée) and escarole are at their best during the cold months of fall and early winter.

GROWING GREENS

ORGANIC AND NONORGANIC

Years ago, all vegetables and fruits were grown organically, because synthetic fertilizers, herbicides, and pesticides had not been developed. When these products began to appear in the first half of the 1900s, farmers embraced them because the crop yields were much larger. In the second half of the 1900s, a small movement back to organic production began, and by the 1980s, high-end restaurants were using organic produce with increasing frequency. By the mid-1990s, customer demand had become so strong that large supermarket chains began devoting a part of their produce sections to organics. Today, organic produce is one of the fastest-growing sectors of the market.

People choose to buy organic greens because they are free of harmful pesticides, herbicides, and fertilizers. They know that organic production methods represent sustainable agriculture and responsible stewardship of the land. In addition, they feel that organically produced greens taste better and are safer to eat.

To be labeled organic, a product must meet the U.S. government standards set forth in the National Organic Program, established in 2001. Nonorganic greens are not subject to the same regulations and can be grown in a wide variety of ways.

HEIRLOOMS AND HYBRIDS

Heirloom varieties of vegetables are classified as those that were introduced into commerce fifty or more years ago. They are open-pollinated varieties, which means that the different plants freely pollinate each other to produce seed for the next generation, so they contain some genetic diversity within the variety. Generally, heirloom vegetables were grown year after year, because of their good flavor.

In the 1900s, modern plant breeders developed varieties that solved problems for growers but did not necessarily focus on flavor. These new varieties were resistant to disease, matured early or evenly, responded to synthetic fertilizers, and were more shippable. Many were hybrids, bred from male and female varieties selected to have specific, desirable characteristics. As a result, the produce from the hybrid varieties are extremely uniform, but they don't develop seed for the next generation that is true to type—that is, seeds that will produce plants like the parents. Consequently, both the genetic diversity and the flavor were diminished.

As growers cultivated and became enthused about the new varieties, they abandoned many of the flavorful heirlooms in favor of the new hybrids. When the organic movement began to swell slowly in the 1960s, some heirloom varieties reappeared. In the 1980s, more varieties were available in quantity, and by the turn of the century, they were coming back into mainstream production as flavor and diversity again found value.

Many of today's popular greens are heirlooms. Among them are mâche, which was not commercially available in quantity in this country until 1999, and Lacinato kale, which was unknown in our large markets until around 1995. Several varieties of lettuces, including Merveille de Quatre Saisons, Rouge d'Hiver, Deer Tongue, Lollo Rossa, and Fine Marâichère, along with Fine de Louviers frisée—all mainstays of today's growers—were not cultivated on a large scale until the early 1990s. From Asia we now have such heirlooms as red mustard, mizuna, and a wide range of cabbages that are part of most mesclun or field mixes found in our supermarkets. To find out which greens are heirlooms, I suggest perusing seed catalogs favored by market growers and home gardeners, even if you have no intention of gardening, because these catalogs indicate heirloom varieties.

HYDROPONIC GROWING

With hydroponic production, greens are grown in nutritional solutions, generally in a greenhouse, rather than in the soil. While the resulting greens can be attractive in appearance, hydroponic products do not compare favorably with field greens in terms of taste. The consensus among chefs is that fresh, seasonal field greens are preferable whenever they are available.

SUBSTITUTIONS

It may be that your market is out of a particular green or that what is available isn't the quality you want. Since many greens have similar characteristics and respond in similar ways when used as an ingredient, either cooked or raw, it is helpful to know which greens can be successfully substituted. For this purpose, greens can be broken into three general categories: sturdy greens, tender greens, and lettuces.

STURDY GREENS

Sturdy greens have thickish rather than thin leaves, heavy stems or midribs, and a pronounced flavor. Some, such as chard and kale, are typically eaten cooked, not raw. The chicories, cabbage, and bok choy are also sturdy greens but, unlike chard and kale, are excellent when eaten raw. Because of their sturdy leaves, the chicories, cabbage and bok choy stand up well to grilling, braising, and sautéing.

Suggested Substitutions

BOK CHOY. Both Savoy and green cabbage are good stand-ins for bok choy. A little spinach might be added to the cabbage to replicate bok choy's green leaves.

CABBAGE. Bok choy might be used instead of cabbage in either raw or cooked dishes. In place of cooked cabbage, consider chard as well.

CHARD. Kale is a good substitute for chard, but cook it about 15 minutes longer than chard. Spinach can also stand in for chard, as its flavor and texture are similar, but cook spinach for only 2 to 3 minutes.

CHICORIES, INCLUDING RADICCHIO, ESCAROLE, CURLY ENDIVE (FRISÉE), AND BELGIAN ENDIVE. Because radicchio is often added for its color as well as for its flavor, any of the chicories can be substituted for each other in either raw or cooked dishes.

KALE. Chard is the best substitute for kale because these greens are similar in texture and flavor. Cook chard about 15 minutes less than kale.

TENDER GREENS

Tender greens have delicate leaves or leaves with a high moisture content. While they are eaten raw, they can be braised, blanched, or added to hot soups at the last minute.

Suggested Substitutions

ARUGULA. In a salad, substitute watercress for a more assertive flavor, mâche or spinach for a milder flavor but similar texture. In a cooked dish, try watercress, but be sure to remove the stems.

MÂCHE. In a salad or cooked dish, baby or young spinach would be the best choice for a mild flavor and tender texture. Baby arugula leaves or watercress could be used as well, but both have a more intense flavor than mâche.

SPINACH. In a salad, consider watercress, arugula, mâche, or a mixture of these greens along with lettuce. In a cooked dish, substitute kale or chard, and cook these for a longer time. Mâche might also be used, but cook it very briefly.

WATERCRESS. In a salad, substitute arugula for the most assertive flavor, mâche or spinach for a milder flavor but similar texture. In a cooked dish, spinach can fill in for the watercress.

LETTUCES

Generally speaking, lettuces are all mild in flavor with a high moisture content. One variety of lettuce can generally be substituted for another. The main difference is in the texture, shape, and color of the leaves, although some types are more flavorful than others. Iceberg and romaine are quite crisp and crunchy, while butterhead and looseleaf lettuces are much softer and more delicate.

Suggested Substitutions

BUTTERHEAD *(also called Bibb)*. If delicate texture is desired, substitute baby spinach.

ICEBERG. Substitute romaine or, depending upon the dish, cabbage. If a firm and crunchy lettuce is not essential, substitute any lettuce.

LOOSELEAF. Substitute romaine or butterhead, spinach, or a combination.

ROMAINE. Substitute a mixture of iceberg for crunch and another type of lettuce for flavor and color.

PREPARING GREENS

Before being used in a salad, leafy greens, such as lettuce, spinach, escarole, frisée, and arugula, should be washed and dried, either in a salad spinner or by gently wrapping them in a dry towel to absorb the water. Depending upon the cooking method, sometimes they are washed but not dried. They can be washed and dried and then stored in plastic bags in the refrigerator, or washed just before using.

Ready-to-use greens, such as mâche, baby arugula, mesclun, and baby spinach, can be lightly sprinkled with water and stored in damp cloth or paper towels or in a plastic bag in the refrigerator until ready to use. This will help to keep them crisp and fresh. For information about storing specific greens, see Chapter 2.

USEFUL TOOLS: SALAD SPINNER, COLANDER, SHARP PARING KNIFE, CHEF'S KNIFE, MANDOLINE, GRATER, BLENDER, FOOD PROCESSOR.

CHIFFONADING. This special slicing technique, which produces ribbons, is accomplished by rolling a leaf into a cigar shape and, using a sharp knife, cutting it crosswise into slices. The slices may be very, very thin, a scant 1/8 inch or larger, depending upon the size you want. Chicories, chard, and spinach are all amenable to this technique.

CHOPPING. A large chef's knife is ideal for chopping greens. Firm-headed greens are usually sliced before chopping. To chop, lay the greens on a work surface. Keeping one hand on top of the knife and the other on the handle, chop in a fan pattern, leaving the tip of the knife on the work surface. Continue chopping until the greens are the desired size.

SLICING. Greens with firm, solid heads, such as iceberg lettuce, cabbage, and radicchio, can be cut into slices using a sharp knife or, for the thinnest slices, a mandoline. With these vegetables, the technique is known as shredding. Before shredding, the heads are generally cut in half or into quarters, depending upon their size. The core of the cabbage is usually removed with a knife before slicing but is left intact for other firm greens.

Looser-headed greens, such as romaine lettuce, escarole, frisée, radicchio, bok choy, and Belgian endive, can be sliced with a knife, crosswise or lengthwise, but are not suitable for slicing with a mandoline since the heads are not solid enough. Thick stems or ribs, such as those of chard and bok choy, are also easily sliced with a knife.

TEARING. Some greens are torn into bite-sized pieces, rather than chopped, for salads. This works especially well for the irregular, loose-headed types with supple leaves, such as lettuces, escarole, frisée, spinach, and radicchio.

COOKING GREENS

Greens are adaptable to a number of cooking methods, and most techniques can be used for most greens, with adjustments made to the cooking time as needed. For example, cabbage, which has thick, rather sturdy leaves, will take longer to wilt than spinach, whose leaves are thin and tender. Regardless of the method, the tender greens, such as spinach, arugula, mâche, watercress, and lettuces, generally take less time to cook than the sturdier greens, such as cabbage, kale, chard, bok choy, and the chicories.

BRAISING. Greens are braised by cooking them slowly in a covered pan with a little liquid until very tender. Sometimes a dish will call for the braised greens to brown by the end of the cooking, while other times, browning will not be desirable. The braising liquids, which add to the character of the greens, can include water; chicken, beef, or vegetable broth; wine; or beer as well as enrichments, such as butter, oil, or cream. Other ingredients, including shallots, onions, and aromatics, can be added as well. Braising may also be done as a preliminary step to using the greens in a gratin or other dish. Depending upon the recipe, the greens may be left whole, halved, or chopped before braising. Braised whole or halved heads of escarole, romaine, bok choy, lettuce, or Belgian endive make an elegant accompaniment to meat and fish. Braised chopped leaves of kale or chard are more rustic, ideal for dressing with olive oil and garlic.

DEEP-FRYING. Deep-frying is a quick-cooking technique in which the greens, with or without batter, are cooked briefly in hot fat—30 seconds for tender greens like spinach or watercress, and 4 to 5 minutes for wedges of radicchio or cabbage. Fat or vegetable oils, which can withstand frying temperatures up to at least 365 degrees F, are used. Deep-frying is most effectively done in a deep-fat fryer, where the temperature of the oil can be controlled, but it can be accomplished in a heavy-bottomed pan on the stovetop. Good choices for deep-frying are greens that will cook quickly yet still retain their shape and flavor. This includes spinach, arugula, watercress, mâche, Belgian endive leaves or quarters, slices or wedges of radicchio and cabbage, and chunks of bok choy. A variety of batters, typically made with milk, flour, and eggs, can be used. Sometimes beer is added for leavening. Batter-dipped deep-fried greens can be served with a selection of other fried vegetables or meats, such as Italian fritto misto or a tempura platter, or as a side dish. A scattering of deep-fried arugula, mâche, or watercress makes a distinctive garnish for soups, or sprinkle them over grilled pork chops, chicken breasts, or mashed potatoes.

GRILLING. With grilling, foods are cooked directly over a hot fire. Firm-headed greens—cabbage, radicchio, and Belgian endive—can be grilled most successfully. Cabbage and radicchio should be sliced, leaving the core intact so the slices won't fall apart during cooking. Cut Belgian endive in half lengthwise or, if they are small, grill them whole. Bok choy, which has firm, solid stalks, also takes well to grilling and can be treated like Belgian endive. Marinate the greens in olive or another vegetable oil and, if desired, season with salt, pepper, and perhaps garlic, herbs, or spices, or simply brush them with butter. Then oil the grate before placing the greens on the hot grill. Grilled greens can be served as a savory side dish for meats, poultry, and fish. They also add complex flavors to other dishes, such as warm salads and pastas.

ROASTING. Because roasting uses dry heat, it is not a common method for preparing greens. Without any skin to protect them while they roast, they would dry out. However, if oiled or provided with some other protection, firm-headed greens, such as cabbage, radicchio, and Belgian endive, can be roasted and will become deliciously tender and moist. These greens, as well as chard, kale, escarole, and frisée, can be added to fish, poultry, or meats as they roast. The roasting juices will baste the greens and infuse them with flavor. Chard and kale cook in about 15 minutes, while escarole and frisée need even less time. Sliced or quartered cabbage, radicchio, and halved Belgian endive may require 30 minutes or longer.

SAUTÉING. Greens are sautéed by cooking them quickly over medium-high or high heat in a little fat to varying degrees of doneness. Seasonings like salt, pepper, fresh herbs, and spices are usually added. Typical fats include butter or oils, such as olive, sunflower, corn, peanut, or walnut, or rendered fat from bacon or duck. When greens are sautéed, a degree of caramelization or browning is often desirable, and they become slightly browned or golden. Because this is a quick-cooking process, the greens are usually cut into thin slices or chopped. Sautéed greens like radicchio, cabbage, kale, or chard may be served on their own or added to other ingredients, such as pasta, beans, or rice. They also combine well with other vegetables, such as roasted red peppers, eggplant, or mushrooms.

STEAMING. One of the simplest methods for cooking greens, steaming keeps their flavors pristine. Use a steamer rack placed over boiling water or a collapsible vegetable steamer insert for a saucepan. Make sure the boiling water does not touch the vegetables. Cooking time varies, with only a few minutes needed for the tender-leaved greens and more for the sturdier greens, such as cabbage, kale, and chard. Steamed greens are often served as a side dish, on their own or with a little seasoning.

STIR-FRYING. Greens are important in classic Asian stir-frying and are either cut into bite-sized pieces or shredded. The heat is high, the fat is hot (usually oil is used because butter burns at high temperatures), and the cooking time is very short. In Asian cooking, bok choy, cabbage, spinach, chard, and kale are all commonly added to stir-fries, but Belgian endive, radicchio, romaine, watercress, and arugula can be used as well.

SWEATING. Greens are sweated by cooking them slowly, usually in butter but sometimes in liquids, such as broth or wine, until they have absorbed all the moisture and are very tender but not browned. Sweating is usually the first step in a preparation, rather than a technique used to create the final dish. Sweated greens, such as cabbage, escarole, or mâche, might then be transformed into a cream soup, a gratin, or a soufflé.

WILTING. Wilting greens involves adding a scant amount of liquid to the pan, covering them, and cooking over medium-high heat just long enough to wilt them, with no browning or crisping. This is a good technique for the tender greens, providing them with enough moisture so they can be warmed through yet still retain their character. Wilted greens, such as arugula, mâche, and spinach, make good beds for warm salads or can be served on their own as a side dish.

OPPOSITE PAGE (*top to bottom*): Stir-fried Napa Cabbage, Bok Choy, and Hot Chiles (page 129), Frisée, Mâche, and Pear Salad with Toasted Pecans (page 77), Skewered Lime and Ginger Prawns with Watercress and Frisée (page 49)

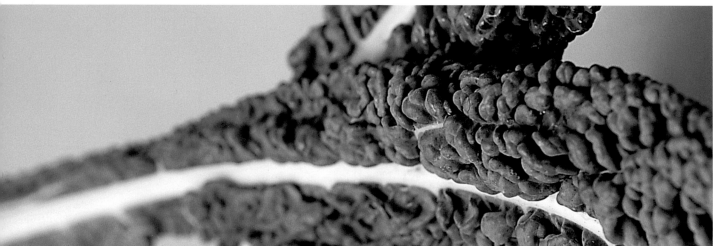

I'VE CHOSEN THESE FOURTEEN GREENS, INCLUDING FOUR MAIN LETTUCE TYPES, BECAUSE THEY REPRESENT THE MOST POPULAR EUROPEAN, ASIAN, AND AMERICAN GREENS IN THE MARKETPLACE.

For each one I have included background information, shopping and storing tips, any special preparation, if needed, plus a goodly amount of nutrition information. If you are a backyard gardener, or would like to be, you'll find here what you need to know to get started growing your own greens, even if you have limited space. OPPOSITE PAGE (*top to bottom*): chicories, kale, cabbages

glossary of greens

ARUGULA

Arugula (*Eruca sativa*). Arugula is the Italian name for this pungent green, which is also known as *roquette* in French and rocket in English. Twenty years ago, arugula was little known in this country outside the Italian community, but market growers started importing the seed and growing it for restaurants. Soon, arugula could be found at farmers' markets, and it is now a common ingredient, available in supermarkets across the country. It is grown in fields as well as indoors in greenhouses, particularly in winter. ‖ Young arugula and mature arugula leaves differ in color, shape, and flavor. Harvested when they are about 2 inches long, young arugula is distinguished by bright green spear-shaped leaves, sometimes with one or two indentations, or notches, at the base. The leaves taste nutty, with a hint of pepper. Mature arugula leaves can grow up to 12 inches long, and they are deep, dark green. Deep notches mark the entire length of the leaves, and their flavor is sharp and pungent, with a healthy bite of pepper. The white flowers are also edible and have a mild, peppery taste. A strain of arugula called wild arugula has edible yellow flowers and grayish-green leaves that are thicker and have a stronger bite than garden arugula. Wild arugula seeds may be purchased, but the greens themselves are rarely available in markets. ‖ Like many greens, arugula can be used raw in salads or cooked in soups, stuffings, sautés, and pasta dishes. SHOPPING. With young arugula, look for bright, clear green leaves. With mature arugula, look for shiny, dark green leaves. Avoid arugula with yellowing or wilting leaves. STORING. Sprinkle lightly with water and store in plastic bags in the refrigerator for up to four days. SPECIAL PREPARATION. With mature arugula, remove the stems and discard or compost. GARDENING. Arugula is easy to grow from seed in the home garden or in containers. A two-foot-square space will provide an adequate supply for most family kitchens. The entire plant may be harvested, or leaves may be cut repeatedly and new ones will grow. NUTRITION. Like almost all leafy greens, arugula is low in calories and high in vitamin C and beta-carotene. Arugula is also a member of the mustard family and thus the larger category of cruciferous vegetables known for their anticarcinogenic effects.

BOK CHOY

Bok Choy (*Brassica rapa* var. *chinensis*). Also called pak choi, bok choy is actually an Asian cabbage, of which there are a number of different types. Most are characterized by dark green, rounded leaves with succulent white midribs that start from a large, bulbous base. The midribs are crunchy and quite mild, while the leaves have a hint of pepper or mustard. Shanghai, or green-stemmed, bok choy is smaller and has a milder flavor than the white-stemmed varieties. Chinese flat cabbage, a bok choy that grows in a flattened rosette shape, exhibits typical bok choy flavors. ‖ In the kitchen, bok choy can be chopped and used raw in salads, especially the tender inner leaves. More often, however, it is sautéed, stir-fried, and added to soups. SHOPPING. Look for upright leaves and crisp stalks that show no cracking or brown edges. STORING. Store in plastic bags in the refrigerator for up to five days. SPECIAL PREPARATION. Trim the base of the stalks before using. GARDENING. Like other cabbages, boy choy is easily grown in the garden, either from seed or from transplants. NUTRITION. Bok choy is a good source of vitamin C, calcium, potassium, and fiber. It shares the anticancer nutritional assets of other cabbages and, unlike its paler relatives, is a rich source of beta-carotene as well, due to its dark green leaves.

Cabbage (*B. oleracea,* var. *capitata*) and Chinese Cabbage (*B. rapa* var. *pekinensis* and *B. rapa* var. *chinensis*). There are dozens of varieties of cabbages, but they all fall into one of two general categories: European or Asian. European cabbages have solidly packed, firm heads, while Asian cabbages are more varied, many with looser leaves and sometimes open heads. European cabbages may be light green, blue green, dark green, or red, with round, conical, or flat heads. Regional favorites can be found in farmers' markets, often with the huge wrapper leaves that protect the head still intact. There are also ornamental cabbages in shades of pink, rose, or purple combined with white or gray-green. In general, European cabbages are more strongly flavored than Asian ones. Asian cabbages technically include what we call bok choy, also called pak choi and pak choy (see Bok Choy, facing page). Here we will consider only the firm-headed types—the barrel-shaped, hearted cabbage, often called nappa or napa cabbage, and the tall, cylindrical "Michili" Chinese cabbages. These cabbages have distinctive shapes; the leaves are usually pale green and crinkly, and become nearly white as the tender center is reached. Napa cabbages, which weigh 3 to 10 pounds, are especially mild and crisp. The Michili types are tall cylinders, up to 18 inches long but only 4 to 6 inches wide. Their darker, sometimes hairy outer leaves taste slightly stronger than napa cab-bage. Loose-headed varieties, which have a slightly mustard flavor, can be found in Asian markets but rarely in supermarkets.

Most cabbages are interchangeable in the kitchen, the differences being more in appearance and texture rather than in flavor. Because Asian cabbages have more delicate leaves and broader ribs than the smooth-leaved European cabbages, Asian varieties cannot withstand long cooking. This is also true for the European Savoy cabbage, which has rather delicate ruffled, or savoyed, leaves. Cabbages can be used raw or cooked and are extremely versatile. Individual leaves and even the whole head can be stuffed. The leaves can be shredded and used raw in salads or added to stews, or the heads can be cut into wedges and braised or grilled. Young leaves of ornamental cabbages are excellent braised but are rarely eaten raw, except for the smallest leaves, as their flavor is strong and their texture coarse. SHOPPING. With European cabbages, look for heavy, solid heads. With Asian cabbages, look for tightly wrapped leaves and weight that is appropriate for the cabbage's size. STORING. Loosely wrap both types of cabbage heads in plastic wrap and store in the refrigerator for up to one week. They are best stored as heads, not as individual leaves. SPECIAL PREPARATION. If the cabbage is to be shredded, first cut it in half, then cut out the hard V-shaped core. If stuffing a whole head, leave the core intact. GARDENING. Cabbages are readily grown from seed or from transplants. There are dozens of varieties from which to choose, and many are selected for planting and harvesting in specific climates and times of the year. Ask your local nursery to suggest cabbages that are best suited for your region. NUTRITION. Cabbage, along with broccoli, cauliflower, Brussels sprouts, and mustard, is a member of the cruciferous family of vegetables, whose specific chemical components appear to reduce the risk of certain forms of cancer; cabbage is most strongly indicated as a deterrent to colon cancer. Cabbage also contains selenium, another known cancer-fighting nutrient found in few other leafy greens. It contains chlorine and sulfur, both beneficial detoxifying minerals, and is a good source of folic acid, fiber, potassium, and vitamin C.

CHARD

Chard *(Beta vulgaris cicla)*. Chard, sometimes called Swiss chard, is a type of beet that has been selected for its leaf development rather than for its root. There are a number of varieties of chard but all share basically the same characteristics of a broad, spear-shaped leaf with savoyed, or ruffled, edges and a pronounced midrib. Some French and Italian varieties may produce leaves up to 3 feet long with midribs as wide as 8 inches, but in markets in the United States, we typically see leaves a third that size, often with very small midribs. The ribs, which are frequently cooked separately from the leaves, may be red, white, pale green, gold, or shades of pink, while the glossy leaves range from deep forest green to apple green. The leaves of red chard have dark crimson tones, those of golden chard, a hint of yellow. Regardless of leaf shape or color, all varieties have an earthy, slightly tart flavor. ‖ Unlike many greens, chard is usually cooked rather than eaten raw, although young, tender leaves find their way into warm tossed salads. The midribs are usually removed before cooking, as they are more fibrous than the leaves and take longer to cook. On their own, diced chard ribs are a delicacy in Mediterranean countries, where they are seasoned with olive oil and garlic and sautéed, or transformed into gratins or other baked dishes. Chard ribs and leaves are stirred into soups and stews, and added to stuffings and pasta dishes. They are also excellent when braised. SHOPPING. Look for glossy, crisp leaves. Avoid chard that is limp and wilted. STORING. Store in plastic bags in the refrigerator for up to five days. SPECIAL PREPARATION. Remove the entire length of the thick midrib and cook it separately, allowing for extra time. GARDENING. Chard may be grown from seed or from transplants in a small space or in containers. Leaves can be cut repeatedly from the plant and new ones will grow. Two or three plants will provide an ample supply for the home cook. NUTRITION. Chard is a good source of beta-carotene, vitamin C, and some B vitamins. It is also high in minerals: iron, potassium, sodium, and magnesium.

CHICORIES

The chicory genus is a diverse group that includes Belgian endive, curly endive (frisée), escarole, red radicchio, and numerous varieties of Italian green chicories. The chicories share the common trait of varying degrees of bitterness, which is part of their appeal. These hardy greens are extremely popular in Europe, especially in the fall through early spring, when more delicate lettuces are in shorter supply. In the kitchen, they are among the most versatile of all the greens. Delicious raw in salads, they are equally good braised, sautéed, or grilled. They can be used in soups, gratins, stews, and pastas, and make especially good side dishes for all kinds of meats. High in vitamin C, all chicories provide a tonic and diuretic effect.

Belgian Endive (*Cichorium intybus*). Belgian endive heads are composed of layers of succulent, pale ivory leaves that form plump, torpedo-shaped heads called chicons. There is also a red variety. Both are characterized by a mildly bitter flavor. However, if exposed to light, the tips of the ivory leaves, which are pale yellow, will turn green and taste unpleasantly bitter. The red variety is less susceptible to this. An excellent addition to salads for its flavor, texture, and color, Belgian endive also makes a superb gratin or braised dish. The crisp leaves can be garnished with spreads and trimmings, such as herbed cheese, smoked fish, or capers. SHOPPING. Look for pale chicons that show no greening on the tips of the leaves and are free of brown spots. STORING. Since Belgian endive is light sensitive, wrap it in opaque paper and store in plastic bags in the refrigerator for up to two weeks. SPECIAL PREPARATION. Remove the bitter core by inserting a sharp knife into the base of the chicon and cutting around the core in a cone shape. GARDENING. Belgian endive is a challenge for the home gardener as it is cultivated in two stages. In the first stage, a large, leafy, very bitter green is grown. Then the leaves are cut off to within 1/2 inch of the crown, and the large roots are dug up. The roots are kept in a dark place for several weeks with a temperature of about 52 degrees F, then buried in sand or kept upright in special plastic containers or bags to force new leaves. In approximately thirty days, the chicons will have formed. NUTRITION. Grown in the dark to keep it mild and white, the Belgian endive does not contain beta-carotene or chlorophyll like its chicory relatives. However, it is a source of considerable potassium, fiber, and some B vitamins. Belgian endive is notable for presence of selenium, a trace mineral important to blood flow and overall metabolic health, and thus protective against heart and circulatory diseases. Selenium has also proven to be anticarcinogenic.

Radicchio *(Cichorium intybus)*. Radicchio, or red heading chicory, was an exotic specialty crop in the United States twenty years ago. Today, it is a commodity, found in supermarkets across the country. The colorful leaves with their white bases and bright magenta, maroon, pink, or speckled surfaces are tightly packed to form a solid head. Although radicchio's flavor is more bitter than that of Belgian endive, escarole, and curly endive, this characteristic, along with its striking color, is why it is considered so desirable as a salad ingredient. Because of its sturdy leaf and tight head structure, radicchio can be sliced for grilling and sautéing. The slices will turn sienna brown, and the flavor will become smoky and slightly caramelized. Radicchio can also be braised, and, like iceberg lettuce, its leaves can be used for wrappers. SHOPPING. Look for heads that feel heavy for their size, with no sign of browning. STORING. Store heads or separated leaves in plastic bags in the refrigerator for up to one week. SPECIAL PREPARATION. Remove and discard or compost any outer leaves that appear damaged. If slicing radicchio for grilling or sautéing, leave a bit of the core intact so the slices will hold together during cooking. GARDENING. Radicchio is easily grown from seed in the home garden. Many varieties will first develop dark green or red outer leaves that are quite bitter. The red and white heads will develop later. In most home gardens, this will occur after the cold weather of fall and winter sets in. The outer leaves will die and form a protective cover over the inner head, resulting in tender leaves with brilliant color. Like all chicories, radicchio is high in vitamin C. NUTRITION. High in magnesium, potassium, and beta-carotene, along with some vitamin C, iron, and calcium, radicchio also has detoxifying properties.

CHICORIES / CURLY ENDIVE + ESCAROLE

Curly Endive *(Frisée) (Cichorium endivia)* and Escarole *(Cichorium endivia)*. The main difference between these sturdy greens is the leaf shape, although escarole tends to be slightly sweeter than curly endive. Curly endive, or frisée, leaves are deeply notched with pointed edges coming from a narrow center, similar to a rib, while escarole has broad, wavy leaves. Both have blanched yellow centers surrounded by dark green outer leaves. The blanched centers, or hearts, are the most desirable part of the head because they are the most tender and mild. In Europe, where these greens are a staple, the heads may reach up to 18 inches in diameter, with 12-inch hearts. There are a number of different varieties, some of which grow upright, but the most common are the round-headed types. Curly endive is a popular salad green because of its taste and its unique lacy appearance. Both escarole and endive have sturdy leaves that stand up well to warm dressings and hearty flavors. They are excellent braised, sautéed, wilted, or stir-fried and adapt to other cooking techniques as well. SHOPPING. Look for heads with the largest blanched centers. STORING. Store heads or separated leaves in plastic bags in the refrigerator for up to five days. SPECIAL PREPARATION. The dark green outer leaves can be quite tough and fibrous, so they may need to be removed and discarded or composted. GARDENING. Escarole and curly endive are quite easily grown from seed in the home garden. To blanch them, gather up the head about one week before harvest and put a rubber band around it to keep the sunlight out and prevent the inner leaves from photosynthesizing. Alternatively, plant the seeds close together. As the plants grow, they will push against one another, sheltering the centers. They can then be harvested by cutting out the centers, which will regrow, or, more traditionally, by harvesting the whole head. NUTRITION. While earning good marks for beta-carotene, fiber, potassium, and iron, this green with curly, almost frilly leaves is an especially rich source of folic acid. Folic acid is a key water-soluble vitamin B complex necessary for production of red blood cells, cell division, and proper brain function. Delicate folic acid is available from fresh, unprocessed foods and is very easily destroyed by light, heat, and time spent in storage, so while a welcome addition to a stir-fry or soup, for optimum nutrition, add curly endive to your salad greens mix.

KALE

Kale *(Brassica oleracea)* (many groups). There are many different kinds of kale, including collards, Scotch, blue, Siberian, ornamental, and Lacinato, or Italian, kale. These hearty greens differ in the shapes and colors of their leaves and in their growing patterns. Collards and Lacinato kale are the tallest, with the most upright growth habits and the longest leaves. Collard leaves are light gray-green with rather heavy stems, and the blue-green Lacinato leaves are long, narrow, and heavily savoyed, looking puffed and quilted. Lacinato is also marketed as Toscano kale, *cavolo nero,* or black cabbage, and Dino, or dinosaur, kale. Ornamental kales, similar to ornamental cabbages, are strikingly beautiful, in shades of bright magenta, deep rose, bright pink, gray-green, and ivory white; their leaves may be curly or deeply serrated. Gray-green Scotch and blue kale are the varieties most commonly seen in markets and have very curly leaves. There is also a new variety that resembles blue kale but is deep magenta. Siberian kale, also called Red Russian kale, produces small, lacy-looking gray leaves veined with pink, attached to pinkish-red stems. It is the tenderest of the kales. Kale is a member of the Brassica family, along with cabbage, and is distinguished by a rather cabbagey flavor with a hint of mustard. Because the leaves are quite thick and fibrous, kale is almost always cooked rather than eaten raw. It is excellent braised, steamed, sautéed, and stir-fried, and is often added to soups, stews, pastas, and baked dishes. Lacinato kale is a classic ingredient in minestrone and imparts a noticeable difference in taste to the soup. Although ornamental kale is often not treated as an edible plant, the young leaves are delicious as well as beautiful when braised, and the truly small ones can be tossed into salads. SHOPPING. Look for crisp leaves. Avoid kale that is limp or has noticeable yellowing or black spots. STORING. Store in plastic bags in the refrigerator for up to one week. SPECIAL PREPARATION. Remove any heavy stems and midribs, and discard or compost them. GARDENING. Kale is easily grown from seed. In the garden, individual leaves can be cut from the plant and new ones will grow. Lacinato kale will grow to nearly 4 feet tall, continually producing new leaves at the top of the plant so that it resembles a miniature palm tree. NUTRITION. Kale is a good source of vitamin A, iron, calcium, and chlorophyll.

LETTUCES

With their light texture, their affinity for dressings, and their ease of use, lettuces are the most popular salad ingredient in the United States. For many years, iceberg and romaine dominated the market, but today there are dozens of varieties, including heirlooms imported from Europe, such as Lollo Rossa, Merveille de Quatre Saisons, and Rouge d'Hiver, as well as new varieties produced by plant breeders, both in the United States and in other countries. There are four general categories of lettuce: crisphead or Batavian butterhead, also called Bibb; romaine; and looseleaf.

LETTUCE / CRISPHEADS

Crispheads form a large, tight head, and the outer, or wrapper, leaves are usually discarded. The most popular crisphead is iceberg, which was developed from the Batavian type. Batavians, very similar in appearance to crispheads, have looser heads and more crinkly leaves, and exhibit a wide range of color, from light green to red. Although the Batavians are very popular in Europe, they are usually found only in farmers' markets in the United States. Butterhead lettuces have small heads surrounded by fine, smooth, loosely gathered leaves, which may be bronze, red, or green. When grown hydroponically in limestone water, this type of lettuce is marketed as Limestone lettuce. Romaine forms tall, upright heads with firm hearts and crunchy leaves. Romaine, too, comes in many colors, but the more delicate reds and bronzes are rarely seen outside farmers' markets. Looseleaf, also called leaf lettuce, has an open, loose shape and no discernible head. Colors vary from bright green to deep red.

LETTUCE / BUTTERHEAD

Butterhead (Bibb) Lettuce *(Lactuca sativa)*. Because it has such smooth, tender leaves, butterhead is the lettuce to use when you want a delicate salad. It is one of the most common simple salads served in France, and you find it in family-style restaurants dressed with a mustard vinaigrette and sometimes tossed with a few chives or a little parsley. Whole heads, loosely tied with kitchen string and gently braised, are a French specialty as well. Because the leaves are so pliable, they make excellent wrappers. The inner leaves from the heart form perfect "cups" for fillings, such as crab, shrimp, or chicken salad. Butterhead lettuces may be red or green and include the magnificent magenta-leaved heirloom, Merveille de Quatre Saisons. SHOPPING. Look for heads that feel heavy for their size, indicating a solid head. Leaves should be bright and free of bruising. STORING. Store heads in plastic bags in the refrigerator for up to five days. Alternatively, remove the leaves from the head, dip them in cold water, and spin or pat dry. Store the leaves in plastic bags in the refrigerator for up to one week. SPECIAL PREPARATION. Handle the leaves gently, as they bruise easily. GARDENING. Butterhead lettuces are easy to grow in the home garden, either from seed or from transplants. NUTRITION. Butterhead lettuces come in colors ranging from light green to dark red, and the darker ones are the more nutritious, being richer in chlorophyll, beta-carotene, and folic acid. Lettuces are typically eaten raw and fresh, so they retain their nutrients better than some cooked vegetables.

Iceberg Lettuce (*Lactuca sativa*). Sometimes called crisphead, iceberg lettuce is the quintessential salad green and sandwich topper in the United States. Its virtue lies in its crisp, firm, crunchy texture. Chopped, shredded, diced, or wedged, iceberg is tossed with every salad dressing imaginable, and millions of hamburgers and sandwiches daily are finished off with iceberg lettuce. Iceberg plays a role in ethnic dishes in this country, too, where it is found on Mexican tostadas and tacos and on top of hot enchiladas. Look for it, too, in Vietnamese and Thai salads and as a garnish to stir into hot noodle soups. Its large, crisp leaves make perfect wraps for meat, fish, and vegetable fillings, hot or chilled. In its heyday in the 1950s and 1960s, iceberg had little competition other than romaine. SHOPPING. Look for heads that feel heavy for their size, a sign of tightly packed leaves. The color of the outer leaves may vary from bright to pale green, depending upon how many of the wrapper leaves, which are darker in color, have been removed. STORING. Store heads in plastic bags in the refrigerator for up to five days. Alternatively, remove the leaves from the head, dip them in cold water, and spin or pat dry. Store the leaves in plastic bags in the refrigerator for up to one week. SPECIAL PREPARATION. Remove any limp or wilted outer leaves, and discard or compost them. GARDENING. Lettuces of all types are easily grown from seed and from transplants. Although all lettuces prefer a cool climate, firm, solid heads of iceberg lettuce are particularly difficult to produce except under optimum conditions. NUTRITION. While it is often thought that darker greens are more nutritious, iceberg lettuce has as much fiber as romaine, and also offers folic acid, vitamin C, iron, potassium, and traces of other minerals.

Looseleaf (Leaf) Lettuce *(Lactuca sativa)*. Looseleaf lettuces are most commonly marketed as red leaf and green leaf. However, there are other varieties of looseleaf, such as the ruffle-leaved Lollo Rosso, and the pointed, deeply indented Red Oak leaf, Green Oak leaf, and Deer Tongue, which are more often found in farmers' markets. All the looseleafs are very versatile and quite flavorful. They make a good base for salads that include other vegetables, such as carrots, cucumbers, tomatoes, onions, or avocados, because the leaves are sturdy enough not to be overwhelmed yet are tender enough to blend well. SHOPPING. Look for heads that have crisp, not wilted, leaves. STORING. Store heads in plastic bags in the refrigerator for up to five days. Alternatively, remove the leaves from the head, dip them in cold water, and spin or pat dry. Store the leaves in plastic bags in the refrigerator for up to one week. SPECIAL PREPARATION. None. GARDENING. Looseleaf lettuces are easy to grow in the home garden, either from seed or from transplants. NUTRITION. While all lettuces have beta-carotene and a good fiber content; generally deeply colored, looseleaf lettuces are especially high in beta-carotene. It also contains chlorophyll, a valuable nutrient present in all greens, that is the basic component of plants' blood. It's important to the health of mucous membranes, has detoxifying properties, and, as the result of the sun's energy, is thought to have revitalizing effects. Looseleaf lettuces also have some calcium, potassium, B vitamins, and vitamin C. Of the two most common forms, red-leaf lettuces contain more vitamin C than the green-leaf varieties.

LETTUCE / ROMAINE

Romaine Lettuce (*Lactuca sativa*). Romaine lettuce, sometimes called Cos, after the Greek island where it originated, is an exceptionally crisp lettuce, with long, upright dark to bright green leaves that enclose an elongated heart of pale yellow. Red romaine, which can vary from very dark red to showing just a tinge of the color, boasts more tender, delicate leaves than other varieties. One of the most popular lettuces in Europe and in the United States, romaine is prized for its crunchy texture and distinct flavor. This lettuce is traditionally sold either as a whole head or as heart of romaine. In recent years, with the increasing amount of ready-to-eat greens available, the leaves can also be found in bulk, whole or chopped, and packaged in plastic bags as well. ‖ Romaine is used primarily in salads and stands up well to bold ingredients like blue cheese, garlic croutons, anchovies, and Parmesan cheese. Caesar salad, known for its robust flavor, is not a true Caesar if it is made with any lettuce other than romaine. The leaves are suitable for dipping into spreads, and the hearts and even whole heads make a delicate braised dish. Romaine can also be added to soups or stews and puréed to lend color as well as flavor. SHOPPING. Look for heavy, firm heads or hearts and crisp leaves. STORING. Store heads in plastic bags in the refrigerator for up to one week. Alternatively, remove the leaves from the head, dip them in cold water, and spin or pat dry. Store the leaves in plastic bags in the refrigerator for up to one week. Sprinkle chopped romaine with a few drops of water and store in plastic bags in the refrigerator for up to four days. SPECIAL PREPARATION. None. GARDENING. Romaine lettuces are easily grown from seed or from transplants in the home garden. The whole head may be harvested, or individual leaves may be cut and new ones will grow. NUTRITION. Romaine contains some calcium, iron, potassium, phosphorus, folic acid, and vitamin C. The medium to dark green color of romaine leaves indicates a high levels of beta-carotene.

MÂCHE

Mâche (*Valerianella locusta*). Also known as lamb's lettuce and corn salad, mâche is a small, tender cluster of dark green leaves with a nutty flavor and silky texture. There are several varieties, some with a spoon or cup-shaped leaf, others with a flat, round leaf. Although it is an important green in Europe, mâche has only recently been produced in volume in the United States, and it is now becoming available in both bulk and prewashed, ready-to-eat packaging. Like the once-unknown arugula and radicchio, it is certain to become a mainstream green. ‖ Mâche is a favorite in all kinds of salads because of its vibrant color and unique shape, flavor, and texture. It combines well with almost any other ingredient, and the leaves stand up to warm dressings and toppings. Extremely versatile, mâche can be used as a primary ingredient in soups, pastas, stuffings, and sandwiches. When cooked, the leaves wilt quickly but retain their bright green color. SHOPPING. Look for bright green, fluffy leaf clusters. STORING. Store in plastic bags in the refrigerator for up to ten days. SPECIAL PREPARATION. None. GARDENING. Mâche can readily be grown in home gardens, but it requires cool temperatures for the seed to germinate and the plant to thrive. NUTRITION. Mâche is impressive among the salad greens for its high beta-carotene content. It also contains some vitamin C, calcium, iron, and fiber.

MESCLUN

Also called "mesclum," mesclun is named for the Provençal word for "mixture." It refers to the eclectic mix of young cultivated and wild greens that has been sold in the open-air markets in and around Nice for many years. The mixture traditionally contains *roquette*, or arugula, a selection of young lettuces in different colors and shapes, young chicories, and chervil. In season, young dandelion, purslane, red poppy leaves, and other wild greens might be added, along with chives, young fennel fronds, other green herbs, and edible flower blossoms. The idea is to achieve a balanced blend of bitter, pungent, and sweet flavors as well as an attractive mixture of shapes, textures, and colors. I know one man from Nice who swears that the true local combination for mesclun contains about 23 different ingredients. In the mid-1980s, mesclun was popularized in the United States, especially in upscale restaurants, and many small organic growers started producing their own signature blends. As the demand increased, larger growers entered the market and began packaging ready-to-use lettuce mixes in plastic bags or shipping it to markets in bulk. Today, various versions of mesclun, also marketed as field greens or baby salad mix, can be found in markets across the country. These blends make quick salad bases for virtually every use and are excellent to keep on hand in the refrigerator. SHOPPING. Look for mixtures that have brightly colored, crisp leaves with no signs of yellowing. STORING. Sprinkle with a few drops of water and store in plastic bags in the refrigerator for up to six days. SPECIAL PREPARATION. None. GARDENING. Mesclun, a mixture of lettuces, herbs, and greens, is easy to grow. Today, many seed companies sell mesclun seed mixtures, or you can blend your own seeds. However, arugula should not be included in the seed mix but rather cultivated separately. Because it grows quickly, it will soon overshadow and eventually outcompete the slower-growing lettuces and chicories. The various mesclun components can also be grown separately and then the leaves mixed in the kitchen.

SPINACH

Spinach (*Spinacia oleracea*). Spinach is a popular and versatile green in both Eastern and Western kitchens. The two principal types are flat-leaved and savoyed, or curly leaf, spinach, which has a sturdier texture than the flat. The flavors—rich and green, slightly sweet, and a little coppery—are virtually identical. Differences between the varieties depend more upon growing conditions and maturity. Baby spinach of both types, washed and ready to use, either packed in bags or sold in bulk, is now readily available in markets across the United States. Exceedingly tender, these young leaves are ideal for salads. There are several tropical greens that are also called spinach but are not *Spinacia oleracea*. These include New Zealand spinach, Chinese spinach, Ceylon or Malabar spinach, and water spinach. They are treated culinarily like spinach and have a similar flavor and texture. Most can be found in Asian markets. Spinach is used both cooked and raw. A favorite in soups and stews, it also adapts well to braising, boiling, steaming, and sautéing. It also can be cooked into savory pies and gratins, and, in some cultures, it is combined with sugar and dried fruit to make a sweet. Raw spinach is used in salads of all kinds and combined with a host of other ingredients, from fish to nuts. SHOPPING. Look for bright, dark green leaves. Avoid spinach with yellowing leaves or slippery stems or leaves. STORING. Store bunched spinach in plastic bags in the refrigerator for up to four days. Alternatively, unbunch the spinach, wash and dry it, and store the leaves in plastic bags in the refrigerator for up to six days. Baby spinach leaves can be stored in plastic bags in the refrigerator for up to five days. SPECIAL PREPARATION. Remove large, prominent stems, and discard or compost them. GARDENING. Spinach is easily grown from seed. The whole plant may be harvested, or the leaves can be continually cut and new ones will grow. A 2 1/2- to 3-foot-square space will provide the home kitchen with plenty of spinach for salad, but a larger area will be needed for the household that wants lots of cooked spinach. NUTRITION. Spinach deserves its reputation as a food that's good for you: It's extremely high in beta-carotene and is a good source of B vitamins, vitamins C and E, and fiber. It also contains more protein than most vegetables. Its most impressive (and most fabled) nutritional asset is its high iron content; there are nearly 2 mg of iron in a single cup.

Watercress *(Nasturtium officinale)*. Watercress boasts a reputation for elegance. Its rounded, dark green leaves taste peppery, similar to the milder flavor of white pepper rather than the bold pungency of black pepper. The stems can be tough and fibrous or tender and delicate, depending upon how the watercress was grown, the weather, and the season. Watercress thrives in cool growing conditions but can get leggy when cultivated in warmer areas. Although a native of Europe, watercress has spread to Asia, where cooks have adapted it for their cuisines. There, the green is usually cooked, typically in soups and stir-fries. In the United States and Europe, watercress is most frequently used in salads, either on its own or in combination with other greens. It is also an ingredient in cooked dishes, such as the classic watercress soup. Watercress is also excellent in sandwiches, from dainty watercress and smoked salmon tea sandwiches to hearty lamb burgers topped with watercress and hot mustard. SHOPPING. Look for abundant leaves that are bright green and crisp. If the watercress is quite stemmy, it may not have many usable leaves or sprigs. Avoid watercress that shows signs of yellowing or blackening or is slippery. STORING. Sprinkle with a few drops of water and store in plastic bags in the refrigerator for up to five days. SPECIAL PREPARATION. Remove leaves and sprigs from large stems, and discard or compost the stems. GARDENING. Watercress is usually grown from rooted cuttings and needs flowing water and good drainage, making it somewhat difficult to grow in home gardens. It is also grown hydroponically. NUTRITION. Particularly high in beta-carotene, calcium, and chlorophyll, watercress also contains some vitamin C, potassium, iron, magnesium, and traces of nearly all the B vitamins. It is a good source of sulfur, a substance found in amino acids that is necessary for the formation of collagen and the maintenance of healthy skin, hair, and nails, and is important to cellular respiration.

glossary of greens

ARUGULA

BOK CHOY

CABBAGE

CHARD

CHICORIES

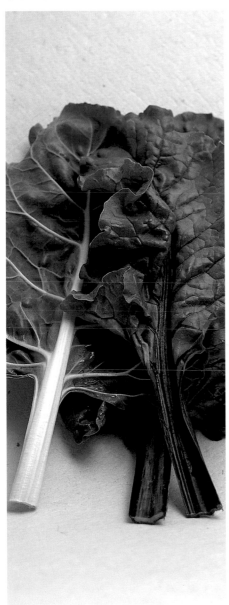

ICEBERG LETTUCE

KALE

MÂCHE

ROMAINE LETTUCE

SPINACH

WATERCRESS

THE SMALL DISHES THAT CONSTITUTE A FIRST COURSE GIVE THE COOK AN OPPORTUNITY TO SET THE STAGE FOR THE MEAL, INTIMATING WHAT WILL FOLLOW. STARTERS MIGHT BE SOPHISTICATED, RUSTIC, OR CASUAL; EVOCATIVE OF THE MEDITERRANEAN, SOUTHEAST ASIA, OR MEXICO; OR SIMPLE DOWN-HOME FARE.

Whatever the style, greens are a wonderful component for starters because their flavors and textures are so distinct, pairing well with everything from fruit to fish. They can be served raw or cooked, warm or at room temperature. Greens might star as the main ingredient, as in Bacon-Wrapped Cabbage Rolls with Blue Cheese and Walnuts. They are equally suitable in a supporting role, as in White Beans with Arugula and Roasted Peppers, where arugula is used as a seasoning.

OPPOSITE PAGE: Radicchio Rolls with Daikon Radish, Cucumber, Crab, and Avocado (page 46)

braised kale with gratinéed potato croutons

1   BUNCH KALE

1   CUP WATER, PLUS MORE AS NEEDED

5   TABLESPOONS EXTRA-VIRGIN OLIVE OIL

1³/4   TO 2 TEASPOONS SALT

2   CLOVES GARLIC, MINCED

2   POTATOES (ANY VARIETY), ABOUT 12 OUNCES TOTAL

2   TEASPOONS HEAVY CREAM OR MILK

1/4   TEASPOON FRESHLY GROUND PEPPER

8   BAGUETTE SLICES, LIGHTLY TOASTED

2   TABLESPOONS FRESHLY GRATED PARMESAN CHEESE

Naturally pungent, kale develops a faintly sweet taste when braised, a flavor that is reflected by the sweet creaminess of the potato topping. This makes an especially appealing appetizer on a winter's night and could be served with prosciutto to add a salty note. Chard or spinach could be substituted for the kale, in which case cooking time would be reduced to 15 minutes for chard and 3 to 4 minutes for the spinach.

Using a sharp knife, cut the stems off the kale and discard. Coarsely chop the leaves (you should have about 6 cups). In a medium saucepan, combine the 1 cup water, 1 tablespoon of the olive oil, 1/2 teaspoon of the salt, and the kale. Bring to a boil over high heat, cover, and reduce the heat to low. Cook, adding more water if necessary, until the kale is so tender you can cut it with a fork, 30 to 40 minutes.

Drain the kale well. In the same saucepan, heat 2 tablespoons of the olive oil, add the garlic, and sauté just long enough to take the raw edge off the garlic, about 45 seconds. Add the kale and sauté, stirring, until it is shiny with olive oil and the garlic is mixed through, 3 to 4 minutes. Keep warm.

Meanwhile, put the potatoes in a medium saucepan and add water to cover by 2 inches. Add 1 teaspoon of the salt and bring to a boil over high heat. Reduce the heat to medium and cook until the potatoes are tender when pierced with a fork, about 20 minutes. Drain the potatoes and let stand until cool enough to handle, about 10 minutes.

Preheat the broiler.

Peel the potatoes and put the flesh in a medium bowl. Add the remaining 2 tablespoons olive oil, the cream, 1/4 teaspoon of the salt, and the pepper and mash until creamy. Taste and add more salt if desired. Spread the potato mixture generously on the toasts, sprinkle with the cheese, and broil just long enough to give the potato mixture a golden finish, 2 to 3 minutes.

Reheat the kale if necessary. Divide the kale equally among 4 small plates and garnish each with 2 potato croutons.

escarole and bay scallop pizzettas
with feta cheese

dough

1	CUP WARM WATER (105 DEGREES F)
1	PACKAGE (1 TABLESPOON) ACTIVE DRY YEAST
1	TEASPOON SUGAR
2 1/2	TO 3 CUPS ALL-PURPOSE FLOUR
1	TEASPOON SALT
3	TABLESPOONS EXTRA-VIRGIN OLIVE OIL
1/4	CUP CORNMEAL

topping

1/4	CUP CHICKEN BROTH
3	CUPS TORN ESCAROLE LEAVES, PALE INNER LEAVES ONLY
3	TABLESPOONS EXTRA-VIRGIN OLIVE OIL
1/3	CUP FRESHLY GRATED PARMESAN CHEESE
6	OUNCES BAY SCALLOPS, RINSED, DRAINED, AND PATTED DRY
4	OUNCES FETA CHEESE, CRUMBLED
2	TEASPOONS DRIED MARJORAM OR OREGANO

Braised Escarole is scattered across a bed of freshly grated Parmesan cheese, then topped with sweet scallops and tangy feta to make an appetizing beginning for a meal. Radicchio, arugula, or kale would be delicious as well.

To make the dough in a food processor: Put the warm water in a small bowl and sprinkle the yeast over it, then the sugar. Let stand until frothy, about 5 minutes. In a food processor, combine 2 1/2 cups of the flour, the salt, 2 tablespoons of the olive oil, and the yeast mixture. Process until a ball forms, about 3 minutes. If too sticky, add a little more flour. Process until the ball is shiny and soft to the touch but no longer sticky.

To make the dough by hand: Dissolve the yeast and sugar in the warm water as directed above. When it is frothy, pour it into a large bowl and add the salt, 2 tablespoons of the olive oil, and half of the flour. Using a wooden spoon, mix the dough, adding more flour until the dough is very stiff.

Turn onto a floured board and knead until the dough is elastic, about 7 minutes. Shape into a ball. Using the remaining 1 table-spoon olive oil, oil a large bowl. Put the dough in the bowl and turn several times to coat. Cover with a damp cloth, set in a warm place, and let rise until doubled, in volume, 1 1/2 to 2 hours.

Preheat the oven to 500 degrees F.

Divide the dough into thirds and roll out each portion into a 10-inch round. Scatter the cornmeal on three 10-inch pizza pans or on 2 baking sheets and transfer the dough rounds to the pans.

To make the topping: In a skillet over medium-high heat, heat the chicken broth. Add the escarole, cover, and reduce the heat to medium-low. Cook until the escarole is limp but still retains its fresh color and the broth has evaporated, 4 to 5 minutes. Remove the escarole and chop coarsely.

Brush each round with some of the olive oil. Scatter with half of the Parmesan cheese, then divide the escarole and the scallops equally among the rounds. Top with the feta cheese and the remaining Parmesan cheese. Bake until the edges and the bottoms of the crusts are golden, about 15 minutes.

Remove the pizzettas from the oven, sprinkle with the marjoram, and drizzle with the remaining olive oil. Cut into wedges and serve hot.

white beans with arugula and roasted peppers

1	LARGE RED BELL PEPPER
1	CUP GREAT NORTHERN BEANS
5	CUPS WATER
1	BAY LEAF
1/2	TEASPOON DRIED THYME
1 1/2 TO 2 TEASPOONS SALT	
2 1/2 CUPS BABY ARUGULA LEAVES, STEMS INTACT, OR MATURE ARUGULA LEAVES, STEMMED	
1	CLOVE GARLIC, FINELY MINCED

2	TABLESPOONS MINCED FRESH FLAT-LEAF PARSLEY
1	TO 1 1/2 TABLESPOONS FRESH LEMON JUICE
1 1/2	TABLESPOONS EXTRA-VIRGIN OLIVE OIL
1/4	TEASPOON RED WINE VINEGAR
1/2	TEASPOON FRESHLY GROUND WHITE OR BLACK PEPPER

Warm beans and smoky bell peppers, laced with garlic and lemon, are seasoned with arugula, then served on a bed of arugula leaves. This rustic dish makes a comforting beginning to a meal. Watercress can be substituted for the arugula.

Put the bell pepper under a preheated broiler, on a grill, or over a direct flame on a gas stove. When one area is charred, turn the pepper and continue charring until it is blackened all over. Put it in a plastic bag and let stand for about 10 minutes. Using your fingers, slip off the charred skin. Stem and seed the pepper and cut into 1/4-inch-thick slices. Reserve 3 slices for garnishing and chop the remaining slices. Set aside.

Meanwhile, pick over and rinse the beans. In a heavy-bottomed, medium saucepan, combine the beans with the water, bay leaf, thyme, and 1 teaspoon of the salt. Bring to a boil over high heat, reduce the heat to low, cover, and simmer until the beans are tender, about 2 hours. Drain the beans and transfer to a large bowl. Finely chop enough of the arugula to make 5 tablespoons and add to the beans along with the garlic, parsley, 1 tablespoon of the lemon juice, the olive oil, vinegar, 1/2 teaspoon of the salt, and the white pepper. Add the chopped bell pepper. Using a wooden spoon, stir gently to distribute the seasonings, being careful not to mash the beans. Taste and add more lemon juice or salt if desired.

Layer the remaining arugula leaves on a platter and mound the warm beans in the center. Garnish with the reserved pepper strips. Serve warm or at room temperature.

radicchio rolls with daikon radish, cucumber, crab, and avocado

6	TABLESPOONS RICE WINE VINEGAR	1	OUNCE FRESH, FROZEN, OR CANNED CRABMEAT, DRAINED WELL IF FROZEN OR CANNED
6	TABLESPOONS LIGHT VEGETABLE OIL		
2	TABLESPOONS CHOPPED FRESH CILANTRO, PLUS 12 SPRIGS FOR GARNISHING	12	LARGE RADICCHIO LEAVES
		12	CHIVES
4	TEASPOONS FRESH LIME JUICE	2	RIPE AVOCADOS, PEELED, PITTED, AND THINLY SLICED
2	TEASPOONS PEELED AND MINCED FRESH GINGER		
1/4	TEASPOON CAYENNE PEPPER		
1/2	CUCUMBER		
1/2	CARROT, PEELED		
1	THREE-INCH-LONG PIECE DAIKON RADISH, PEELED		

Supple, sturdy leaves wrapped around seasoned fillings, cold or warm, are a simple yet elegant first course. Here, shellfish and vegetables are combined, but warm meat fillings, such as spicy sausage with lots of fresh parsley, mint, and cilantro—my favorite— can be used instead. Iceberg lettuce leaves can be substituted for the radicchio and make a brilliant contrast on the plate.

In a medium bowl, combine the vinegar, oil, chopped cilantro, lime juice, ginger, and cayenne and mix well with a fork to make a marinade.

Cut the cucumber half crosswise. Peel one of the pieces, leaving the other unpeeled. Cut both pieces in half lengthwise and, using a metal spoon, scrape out the seeds and discard. Cut both pieces into 1/4-inch-thick matchsticks and put them in the bowl with the marinade. Similarly, cut the carrot and the radish into matchsticks and add them to the marinade. Add the crab and stir to coat all the ingredients with the marinade.

Using a sharp knife or kitchen shears, cut each radicchio leaf into a 4-inch square. Cut the chive stems in half. Reserve the upper pointed ends to tuck into the rolls and the lower ends to make a confetti-like garnish for the platter.

Hold a square of radicchio in your hand and place some of the crab mixture down the center. Top with 2 or 3 avocado slices. Roll up the radicchio to make a cylinder and place the roll, seam-side down, on a platter. Tuck a cilantro sprig and a length of chive in one end. Repeat until all the leaves are filled. Using kitchen shears, clip a sprinkling of the remaining chives, confetti-style, over the lettuce rolls and the bare edges of the platter.

radicchio with smoked salmon, crème fraîche, and capers SERVES 4

¼ CUP CRÈME FRAÎCHE OR SOUR CREAM
8 MEDIUM RADICCHIO LEAVES, CHILLED
6 OUNCES SMOKED SALMON, CUT IN THIN SLICES
1 TABLESPOON CAPERS, DRAINED
2 TABLESPOONS MINCED FRESH CHIVES

Sometimes a very successful first course can be created simply by combining a few ingredients with distinctive flavors into an attractive presentation. This is such a dish. Belgian endive leaves or small romaine lettuce leaves might be used as well.

Put 1 teaspoon of the crème fraîche in the center of each radicchio leaf. Top with one eighth of the smoked salmon, a little dollop of crème fraîche, and one eighth of the capers. Arrange 2 filled leaves on each of 4 plates, then decoratively drizzle the remaining crème fraîche around the outside of the leaves. Scatter the chives across the plates and the leaves and serve immediately.

skewered lime and ginger prawns
with mâche and frisée

prawns

2	TABLESPOONS EXTRA-VIRGIN OLIVE OIL
1/3	CUP FRESH LIME JUICE
1	TABLESPOON PEELED AND GRATED FRESH GINGER
1	TEASPOON RED PEPPER FLAKES
1/4	TEASPOON SALT
1/4	TEASPOON FRESHLY GROUND PEPPER
12	OUNCES MEDIUM PRAWNS (ABOUT 24), PEELED AND DEVEINED (KEEP TAIL SHELLS INTACT)

salad

1	TABLESPOON EXTRA-VIRGIN OLIVE OIL
1	TEASPOON FRESH LIME JUICE
1/2	TEASPOON RICE WINE VINEGAR
1/2	TEASPOON SALT
1/2	TEASPOON FRESHLY GROUND PEPPER
2	CUPS MÂCHE
2	CUPS TORN FRISÉE, PALE INNER LEAVES ONLY
4	WOODEN SKEWERS, SOAKED IN WATER FOR 5 MINUTES

A mixture of crisp and colorful greens can form the base of almost any type of salad. They contrast especially well with hot and spicy ingredients, such as these prawns, seasoned with red pepper flakes and ginger. Spicy chicken, beef, or sea scallops are also delicious. A mesclun mix or watercress makes a fine substitute for the greens.

Prepare a hot charcoal or wood fire in a grill, heat a gas grill, or preheat a broiler.

To prepare the prawns: In a large bowl, combine the olive oil, lime juice, ginger, red pepper flakes, salt, and pepper. Add the prawns and stir to coat. Let stand at room temperature for about 20 minutes.

Meanwhile, make the salad: In a large salad bowl, combine the olive oil, lime juice, vinegar, salt, and pepper and mix well with a fork. Add the mâche and frisée but do not toss. Set aside.

Divide the prawns evenly among the skewers, placing them close together. Oil the grill with a little vegetable oil, then grill the prawns just until firm and opaque, 2 to 3 minutes on each side. Or broil for about 4 minutes on each side.

Toss the salad to coat well with the dressing. Divide equally among 4 salad plates. Place a hot skewer atop each salad. Serve immediately.

seared ahi tuna with watercress and mustard vinaigrette

2	EGGS
2	TABLESPOONS EXTRA-VIRGIN OLIVE OIL
2	TEASPOONS CHAMPAGNE VINEGAR
1/2	TEASPOON DIJON MUSTARD
1¼	TEASPOONS FRESHLY GROUND PEPPER
1/2	TEASPOON SALT
3	CUPS WATERCRESS LEAVES AND TENDER SPRIGS (1 TO 1½ BUNCHES)
12	OUNCES SASHIMI-QUALITY AHI TUNA, ABOUT 1 INCH THICK

The peppery flavor of bright green watercress mirrors the light pepper crust on the tuna. A mustard vinaigrette, its heat tamed by the champagne vinegar, binds the flavors together to create a simple bistro-style first course. Mâche, baby spinach, arugula, or mesclun could be used instead of watercress.

Put the eggs in a saucepan, cover with cold water, and bring to a boil over high heat. Remove the pan from the heat and let the eggs stand in the hot water for 15 minutes. Drain and let cool in the empty pan for 15 minutes, then peel the eggs and set aside.

In a large salad bowl, combine the olive oil and vinegar and mix well with a fork. Add the mustard, 1/2 teaspoon of the pepper, and the salt and mix to make a thick vinaigrette. Transfer about half of the vinaigrette to a small bowl and set aside. Add the watercress to the salad bowl and toss to coat well with the vinaigrette. Divide the watercress equally among 4 salad plates.

Gently press the remaining 3/4 teaspoon pepper onto both sides of the tuna. Heat a dry skillet over high heat. When it is hot, sear the tuna until about 1/4 inch of the red meat turns opaque, about 1 minute. Turn and sear the other side for about 1 minute. At this point, the tuna will be hot on the outside and still cold on the inside. For this dish to be most flavorful, the center of the tuna should be quite rare. However, if you prefer your tuna more done, simply sear longer. Transfer the tuna to a cutting board and, using a very sharp knife, cut into 1/4-inch-thick slices.

Fan 3 or 4 slices of the tuna, slightly overlapping, over each mound of watercress. Cut the eggs in half lengthwise and divide among the plates. Drizzle a little of the reserved vinaigrette over the tuna. Serve immediately.

seared quail with mâche and chanterelle mushrooms

1	HALF-INCH PIECE CINNAMON STICK	1	CLOVE GARLIC, MINCED
1½	TEASPOONS SALT	3	OUNCES CHANTERELLE MUSHROOMS, SMALL ONES LEFT WHOLE, LARGER ONES HALVED OR QUARTERED LENGTHWISE, OR A MIX OF MUSHROOMS, SUCH AS PORTOBELLO, OYSTER, AND SHIITAKE
1½	TEASPOONS PEPPERCORNS		
4	WHOLE CLOVES		
¼	TEASPOON FRESHLY GRATED NUTMEG PINCH OF CARDAMOM	3	OUNCES WHITE OR BROWN MUSHROOMS, THINLY SLICED
4	QUAIL	3	TABLESPOONS DRY WHITE WINE
2	TABLESPOONS EXTRA-VIRGIN OLIVE OIL	¼	CUP CHICKEN BROTH
1	TABLESPOON UNSALTED BUTTER	4	CUPS MÂCHE
2	TABLESPOONS MINCED SHALLOT		

Mâche mixed with warm sautéed mushrooms forms a luscious bed for this quail, which has undertones of North African and Middle Eastern spices. Watercress, baby spinach, baby arugula, or a mesclun mix could be used instead of mâche.

Preheat the oven to 250 degrees F.

In a spice grinder or a clean coffee grinder, grind the cinnamon stick to a coarse powder. Put a scant 1/2 teaspoon in a small bowl and store the rest for another use. Put the salt, peppercorns, and cloves in the grinder and grind to a coarse powder. Combine this powder with the cinnamon, and stir in the nutmeg and cardamom. Using kitchen shears or a knife, cut the quail in half lengthwise. Rub the quail with about two thirds of the spice mixture.

In a large skillet over medium-high heat, heat the olive oil. Add the quail, skin-side down, and fry until the skin is lightly golden, about 3 minutes. Turn and fry the other side until golden, about 3 minutes. Reduce the heat to medium, turn the quail again, and cook until the skin is crisp and golden, about 4 minutes. Turn and cook the other side for about 4 minutes. To check for doneness, insert the tip of a sharp knife into the thickest part of the breast, near the wing. The juices should run clear. Transfer the quail to a warmed ovenproof platter, cover loosely with aluminum foil, and place in the oven.

In the same skillet, melt the 1 tablespoon butter over medium heat. When the butter foams, add the shallot and garlic and sauté until the shallot is just translucent, about 45 seconds. Add the mushrooms and sauté until they are shiny and slightly soft, about 2 minutes. Cover, reduce the heat to low, and cook until the mushrooms are soft and have released their juices, 1 to 2 minutes more. Uncover, sprinkle the mushrooms with the remaining one third of the spice mixture, and stir. Increase the heat to high, add the wine, and cook, stirring to scrape up any bits that cling to the bottom of the pan. Add the chicken broth, reduce the heat to medium, and cook until the liquid is nearly evaporated, about 2 minutes.

Put the mâche in a large salad bowl and add the hot mushrooms, tossing to distribute the mushrooms and wilt the mâche. Divide equally among 4 plates.

Place 2 quail halves, one side propped against the other, on each mound of mâche and mushrooms. Serve immediately.

duck breast with greens and pine nuts

3 TABLESPOONS EXTRA-VIRGIN OLIVE OIL

2 TABLESPOONS RED WINE VINEGAR

1 TEASPOON BALSAMIC VINEGAR

1 TEASPOON SALT

1/2 TEASPOON FRESHLY GROUND PEPPER

2 HEADS BELGIAN ENDIVE

1 CUP BABY ARUGULA LEAVES, STEMS INTACT,
OR MATURE ARUGULA LEAVES, STEMMED AND
LEAVES COARSELY CHOPPED

1 CUP TORN FRISÉE, PALE INNER LEAVES ONLY

1/4 CUP FRESH FLAT-LEAF PARSLEY LEAVES

1/2 CUP PINE NUTS

1 WHOLE BONELESS DUCK BREAST
OR 2 DUCK BREAST HALVES

Thanks to their diverse colors, shapes, and flavors, greens give cooks the opportunity to construct dishes that tempt the eye as well as the palate. They also provide a background for other ingredients—in this recipe, thinly sliced duck—and contribute to the taste of the finished dish. Here this is accomplished with dark green arugula, thin slivers of ivory-colored Belgian endive, and curls of pale-yellow frisée. You could create an equally beautiful presentation using sprigs of watercress or mâche instead of arugula, and radicchio instead of Belgian endive or frisée. Or substitute a mesclun mix.

In a large salad bowl, combine the olive oil, red wine and balsamic vinegars, 1/2 teaspoon of the salt, and the pepper and mix well with a fork.

Using a small, sharp knife, cut an inverted V in the base of each Belgian endive to remove the core. Cut the endive lengthwise into 1/4-inch-wide slivers. Add the endive, arugula, frisée, and parsley to the bowl but do not toss. Set aside.

In a dry small skillet over medium heat, toast the pine nuts, stirring constantly, until they are faint gold, about 5 minutes. Set aside.

Put the remaining 1/2 teaspoon salt in a skillet large enough to hold the duck breast and heat over high heat. When the pan is hot, add the duck breast, skin side down. Reduce the heat to medium-high and cook until the skin is crispy and golden, 6 to 7 minutes. Turn and cook the other side until lightly browned, about 4 minutes. Cover and cook until the duck breast is medium-rare, 3 to 4 minutes longer. Transfer to a cutting board and let stand for 3 to 4 minutes. If you used a whole duck breast, cut it in half. Slice each half diagonally, across the grain, into slices 1/4 inch thick.

Toss the salad to coat well with the dressing and mound it onto a platter. Arrange the warm duck breast slices on top and drizzle with any accumulated juices from the platter. Scatter the pine nuts on top and serve immediately.

bacon-wrapped cabbage rolls with blue cheese and walnuts   SERVES 4

4   MEDIUM GREEN CABBAGE LEAVES

4   APPLEWOOD-SMOKED BACON SLICES

1/4   CUP WALNUTS, CHOPPED

4   OUNCES SOFT BLUE CHEESE, SUCH AS COSTELLO,
    POINT REYES BLUE, OR GORGONZOLA

2   TABLESPOONS MINCED FRESH FLAT-LEAF PARSLEY

This surprisingly simple first course is made with humble ingredients, yet it boasts sophisticated flavors. Savoy or red cabbage might be used, also, and a combination of two or more different types makes a striking presentation.

In a steamer rack set over boiling water, steam the cabbage leaves until softened but not completely limp, about 2 minutes. Cut off the thick base of each leaf, making a straight, rather than a curved, end.

In a medium skillet over medium heat, fry the bacon, turning the slices several times, until they have begun to brown slightly but are still supple, about 5 minutes. Transfer to paper towels to drain.

In a small bowl, mix together the walnuts and cheese.

Preheat the broiler.

Spread about 2 tablespoons of the cheese mixture down the center of each cabbage leaf, to within 1/2 inch of the ends. Starting at the long end, roll each leaf snugly. Wrap a piece of bacon in a spiral fashion around each cabbage roll, fastening both ends of the bacon with a toothpick.

Set the rolls side-by-side in a baking dish just large enough to hold them and broil until the bacon is crisp. Place 1 cabbage roll on each of 4 salad plates and scatter with the confetti-like parsley. Cut each roll into 3 or 4 slices. Serve immediately.

GREENS CAN FORM THE BASIS OF A SOUP, AS IN ESCAROLE SOUP, OR THEY CAN SERVE AS AN ESSENTIAL COMPONENT, AS IN CHOWDERS AND NOODLE SOUPS. THEY ARE ESPECIALLY IMPORTANT IN SOUPS NOT ONLY FOR THE FLAVOR THEY PROVIDE BUT ALSO BECAUSE THEY ARE VISUALLY APPEALING.

Because virtually every culture incorporates greens into soups, cooks have a lot of opportunity to substitute one green for another in recipes. ‖ Delicate greens like spinach, mâche, watercress, and arugula can be used interchangeably, and each will impart a unique taste to the soup. Sturdier greens like escarole, frisée, kale, bok choy, and cabbage all have distinctive flavors, so these greens can define a soup when added in quantity. Raw greens can be stirred into soups as a garnish, providing contrasting texture as well as flavor and an attractive appearance. OPPOSITE PAGE: Mâche and Parmesan Soup (page 59)

watercress soup

2   TABLESPOONS UNSALTED BUTTER

2   SHALLOTS, FINELY CHOPPED

4   CUPS STEMMED WATERCRESS LEAVES

6   CUPS CHICKEN BROTH

1/4 TEASPOON SALT

1/4 TEASPOON FRESHLY GROUND PEPPER

2   TABLESPOONS CRÈME FRAÎCHE OR SOUR CREAM

2   TEASPOONS SNIPPED FRESH CHIVES

Although this classic soup has many variations, the key element is the enticing sharp flavor of the watercress tempered by butter. This recipe was given to me by a French woman, who said it's an easy one she learned from her mother. The watercress is cooked only briefly, then the soup is enriched with crème fraîche just before serving and garnished with snippets of chives.

In a large saucepan over medium heat, melt the butter. When it foams, add the shallots and sauté until translucent, 2 to 3 minutes. Add the watercress and stir until wilted, about 45 seconds, then pour in the chicken broth and bring to a simmer. Stir in the salt and pepper and remove from the heat. Stir in the crème fraîche.

Ladle the soup into soup bowls and garnish with a sprinkling of chives.

mâche and parmesan soup

4   BAGUETTE OR OTHER STURDY COUNTRY
    BREAD SLICES

1½ TABLESPOONS EXTRA-VIRGIN OLIVE OIL

1   CLOVE GARLIC, PEELED

4   CUPS CHICKEN BROTH

2   TABLESPOONS DRY WHITE WINE

1   ONE-OUNCE CHUNK PARMESAN CHEESE
    WITH RIND, PLUS ¼ CUP FRESHLY GRATED
    PARMESAN CHEESE

1   CUP MÂCHE

Light yet with full-bodied flavor, this soup comes together quickly. The mâche wilts into the soup, retaining its petal shape and slightly nutty taste, while the Parmesan contributes complexity to the broth. Serving the soup spooned over garlicky Parmesan-topped toast adds body and texture. Watercress or baby arugula can be used instead of mâche.

Preheat the broiler.

Put the baguette slices on a broiler pan and broil until golden, 5 to 7 minutes. Remove from the broiler and drizzle with the olive oil. Rub the garlic across the surface of the toast slices. The irregular, crisp surface of the toast acts like a grater. Set aside.

In a medium saucepan over high heat, combine the chicken broth and wine and bring to a boil. Boil until reduced by 1 or 2 tablespoons, about 2 minutes. Add the chunk of cheese and reduce the heat to low. Cover and simmer until the cheese has melted a bit and the broth is flavored by it, about 25 minutes. Add the mâche and cook for 2 minutes. Remove the chunk of rind and discard.

Place 1 piece of toast in each soup bowl. Sprinkle each toast with 1 tablespoon of the grated cheese, then ladle the soup over the toast.

cream of escarole soup with chestnuts

1/2 CUP (1 STICK) UNSALTED BUTTER

2 SHALLOTS, DICED

2 CELERY STALKS, DICED

1 SMALL HEAD ESCAROLE, COARSELY CHOPPED (ABOUT 4 CUPS); RESERVE 1 PALE INNER LEAF FOR GARNISHING

1 POUND FROZEN CHESTNUTS, HEATED AS DIRECTED ON THE PACKAGE, 1 POUND UNSWEETENED CANNED OR VACUUM-PACKED CHESTNUTS, OR 2 POUNDS FRESH CHESTNUTS ROASTED AND PEELED; RESERVE 4 CHESTNUTS FOR GARNISHING

1 CUP HEAVY CREAM

3 CUPS CHICKEN BROTH

2 TABLESPOONS DRY SHERRY

1/2 TEASPOON FRESHLY GROUND WHITE PEPPER

1/4 TO 1/2 TEASPOON SALT

Creamy and delicate, yet with a haunting, wild taste of the forest, this elegant soup is easy to make. It reflects the esteem with which even the most humble ingredients are held in France and Italy, where escarole and chestnuts are commonplace. The hearty, slightly bitter flavor of the escarole is balanced by the sweet richness of the chestnuts, creating a truly memorable soup. Fresh chestnuts are available only in fall and winter, but unsweetened frozen, canned, or vacuum-packed chestnuts are sold year-round. Certainly, if you have fresh chestnuts, roast and peel them for your soup.

In a medium saucepan over medium heat, melt the butter. When it foams, add the shallots, celery, and chopped escarole. Reduce the heat to low, cover, and let the vegetables cook slowly without browning for about 5 minutes. Add all but the 4 reserved chestnuts. Continue cooking, uncovered, until the shallots and celery are translucent, the escarole is shiny and limp, and the chestnuts are soft, 5 to 7 minutes longer. Add the cream and chicken broth and simmer, uncovered, until the flavors are blended, about 10 minutes. Remove from the heat.

In a blender or food processor, purée the soup in batches. It should be as smooth and creamy as possible. Strain the soup through a fine sieve into a clean saucepan to remove any bits of vegetables or chestnuts. The soup will now be velvet-smooth. Stir in the sherry.

Reheat the soup gently over low heat but do not boil, as this will spoil the texture. Stir in the white pepper and 1/4 teaspoon of the salt. Taste and add more salt if desired.

Cut the reserved escarole leaf into chiffonade. Slice the reserved chestnuts lengthwise into thin slices.

Ladle the soup into soup bowls, garnish with a few threads of the escarole, about 1 teaspoon per bowl, and 3 or 4 chestnut slices.

kale and potato soup with spicy sausage

12 OUNCES KALE

8   OUNCES CHORIZO OR OTHER SPICY LINK SAUSAGES

3   BOILING POTATOES, SUCH AS RED OR WHITE ROSE
    OR YUKON GOLD, ABOUT 1 POUND TOTAL, PEELED
    AND CUT INTO 1/2-INCH SLICES

1   TEASPOON SALT, PLUS MORE AS NEEDED

5   CUPS CHICKEN BROTH

1/2 TEASPOON FRESHLY GROUND PEPPER

4   BAGUETTE SLICES, LIGHTLY TOASTED

Kale is a key ingredient in this traditional Portuguese soup. In this version, it is thick and creamy, with chunks of sausage. The kale, which has a pronounced flavor, is minced and stirred into the soup. The bits of green give every spoonful a rich and satisfying taste without being overpowering.

Using a sharp knife, cut the stems off the kale and discard. Mince the leaves and set aside.

Using a fork, prick the sausages in several places. Put them in a medium skillet and add water to cover. Bring to a boil over high heat, reduce the heat to low, and simmer for about 15 minutes. Transfer the sausages to a cutting board and cut into 1/4-inch-thick slices. Set aside.

Put the potatoes in a medium saucepan and add water to cover by about 1 inch. Add the 1 teaspoon salt and bring to a boil over high heat. Reduce the heat to medium and cook until the potatoes are tender when pierced with a fork, 10 to 15 minutes. Drain the potatoes, reserving the cooking water.

Put the potatoes in a blender or food processor and purée, slowly adding about 2 tablespoons of the cooking water, to make a very thick, almost sticky paste. Add a little more water if necessary to produce the proper consistency.

In a large saucepan over medium-high heat, combine the kale and chicken broth and simmer for 5 minutes. Stir in the potato paste, pepper, and the sausages. Simmer for 3 to 4 minutes. Taste and add more salt if desired.

To serve, place 1 toasted baguette slice in each soup bowl. Ladle the soup over the toast and serve immediately.

corn and spinach chowder with avocado

red pepper cream

2	LARGE RED BELL PEPPERS
2	TABLESPOONS FRESH OREGANO LEAVES
2	TABLESPOONS CALIFORNIA CHILI OR OTHER MILD CHILI POWDER
1/2	TEASPOON SALT
1	TABLESPOON EXTRA-VIRGIN OLIVE OIL
2	TABLESPOONS HEAVY CREAM

soup

2	BACON SLICES, CHOPPED
1/2	CELERY STALK, DICED (ABOUT 1/4 CUP)
1/2	LARGE ONION, DICED (ABOUT 1/2 CUP)

2	CUPS CHICKEN BROTH
4	OR 5 NEW RED POTATOES, ABOUT 1 POUND TOTAL, CUT INTO 1/2-INCH CUBES
2	TABLESPOONS FRESH THYME LEAVES
2	BAY LEAVES
1/4	TO 1/2 TEASPOON SALT
1/4	TEASPOON FRESHLY GROUND PEPPER
2	CUPS HOT MILK
3 1/2	CUPS CORN KERNELS (YELLOW, WHITE, OR A COMBINATION)
1	CUP CHOPPED STEMMED SPINACH
2	RIPE AVOCADOS, PEELED, PITTED, AND THINLY SLICED

This soup captures the essence of summer. Bursting with the flavors of corn mingled with bright spinach greens, it's topped with a garnish of sweet red pepper cream and avocado slices. Finely chopped chard, with the midribs removed, can be substituted for the spinach.

Preheat the broiler.

To make the red pepper cream: Put the bell peppers under the broiler, on a grill, or over a direct flame on a gas stove. When one area is charred, turn the peppers and continue charring until they are blackened all over. Put them in a plastic bag and let stand for about 10 minutes. Using your fingers, slip off the charred skin. Stem and seed the peppers and coarsely chop them. Put them in a blender with the oregano, chili powder, salt, and olive oil and purée until smooth. Transfer the mixture to a bowl and stir in the cream.

To make the soup: Set a large, heavy-bottomed saucepan or a soup pot over medium-high heat. When it is hot, reduce the heat to low and fry the bacon, stirring, until it has rendered its fat and the meat is crisp, 7 to 8 minutes. Using a slotted spoon, remove the bacon and reserve for another use. Reserve the fat in the pan.

Add the celery and onion to the pan and sauté over low heat until nearly translucent, 3 to 4 minutes. Increase the heat to medium-high, pour in the chicken broth, and stir to scrape up any bits that cling to the bottom of the pan.

Add the potatoes, thyme, bay leaves, 1/4 teaspoon of the salt, and the pepper. Bring to a boil, cover, and reduce the heat to low. Simmer until the potatoes are tender, 12 to 15 minutes.

Add the milk and simmer for 5 minutes. Add the corn kernels and spinach and simmer for 3 to 4 minutes longer. Taste and add more salt if desired. Remove the bay leaves and discard.

Ladle the soup into soup bowls, swirl a spoonful of the red pepper cream into each, and garnish with several avocado slices.

hot-and-sour soup with spinach

6   CUPS CHICKEN BROTH

6   OUNCES WHITE MUSHROOMS, THINLY SLICED

1   BUNCH SPINACH, STEMMED AND LEAVES CHOPPED
    (ABOUT 1½ CUPS)

3   TABLESPOONS LIGHT SOY SAUCE

3   TABLESPOONS RICE WINE VINEGAR

¾   TABLESPOON FRESHLY GROUND PEPPER

2   TEASPOONS SESAME OIL

½   TEASPOON HOT CHILE OIL

5   OUNCES FIRM TOFU, CUT INTO ½-INCH CUBES

5   TABLESPOONS WATER MIXED
    WITH 3 TABLESPOONS CORNSTARCH

1   EGG, BEATEN

¼   CUP CHOPPED FRESH CILANTRO

2   GREEN ONIONS, INCLUDING HALF
    OF THE GREEN PART, MINCED

Adding greens to hot-and-sour soup gives it a substantial texture and enhances the flavor. This recipe calls for spinach, although julienned chard, mâche, watercress, or cabbage could be used instead. The soup is nice and peppery, which I like, but if you prefer a milder version, simply cut back on the black pepper.

In a large saucepan or a soup pot over high heat, bring the chicken broth to a boil. Reduce the heat to medium, add the mushrooms and spinach, and simmer for 5 minutes. Add the soy sauce, vinegar, pepper, sesame oil, chile oil, and tofu and stir. Then stir in the water and cornstarch mixture and the egg, and cook for 1 minute.

Ladle the soup into soup bowls, and garnish with the cilantro and green onions.

miso soup with watercress and slivered root vegetables

6   CUPS WATER

2   TABLESPOONS WHITE MISO

2   OUNCES SMALL WHITE MUSHROOMS, HALVED

1   SMALL CARROT, PEELED AND JULIENNED

1   THREE-INCH-LONG PIECE DAIKON RADISH,
    JULIENNED

3   OUNCES FIRM TOFU, CUT INTO $1/2$-INCH CUBES

1   CUP STEMMED WATERCRESS LEAVES

The watercress leaves, which serve as a garnish, contribute a hint of pepper to this delicate miso soup. Miso is a bean paste made by fermenting soybeans with other ingredients and is commonly used as a flavoring in Asian cooking, much like soy sauce. Mâche, bok choy leaves, or baby spinach can be substituted for the watercress.

In a saucepan over medium-high heat, bring the water to a boil. Stir in the miso and reduce the heat to medium. Stir in the mushrooms, carrot, daikon radish, and tofu. Cook until the vegetables are tender, about 5 minutes. Remove from the heat. Ladle the soup into soup bowls and garnish each with one fourth of the watercress leaves. Serve immediately.

asian noodle soup with bok choy and shiitake mushrooms

6   CUPS WATER

9   OUNCES FRESH UDON NOODLES

4   CUPS CHICKEN BROTH

2   TABLESPOONS LIGHT SOY SAUCE

1   TEASPOON PLUM SAUCE

4   GREEN ONIONS, INCLUDING ABOUT ONE FOURTH OF
    THE GREEN PART, THINLY SLICED ON THE DIAGONAL

4   OUNCES SHIITAKE MUSHROOMS, STEMMED
    AND THINLY SLICED

2   CUPS COARSELY CHOPPED BOK CHOY LEAVES
    (GREENS ONLY)

This soup is truly quick and simple to prepare. The noodles and broth take only a few minutes to cook, and the bok choy and mushrooms are stirred in at the very end to produce a rich, vegetable-laden soup. Finely shredded cabbage or chopped spinach can fill in for the bok choy.

In a medium saucepan over high heat, bring the water to a boil. Add the noodles and cook until soft, about 3 minutes. Drain and rinse in cold water. Set aside.

In a medium saucepan over medium-high heat, combine the chicken broth, soy sauce, plum sauce, and green onions. Bring to a boil, then reduce the heat to low and simmer for 5 minutes to allow the flavors to blend. Add the mushrooms and simmer until they are soft, 2 to 3 minutes. Add the noodles and bok choy and simmer until the bok choy is just wilted, about 1 minute. Remove from the heat and ladle the soup into soup bowls.

chard and lentil soup with duck confit

6	CHARD LEAVES	1/2	TEASPOON FRESHLY GROUND PEPPER
2	TEASPOONS, PLUS 1/4 CUP EXTRA-VIRGIN OLIVE OIL	2	DUCK LEGS CONFIT
1	MEDIUM YELLOW ONION, MINCED	8	BAGUETTE OR OTHER STURDY COUNTRY BREAD SLICES, EACH 1/2 INCH THICK
1	CLOVE GARLIC, MINCED		
1	CARROT, PEELED AND MINCED		
2	CUPS LENTILS		
10	CUPS WATER		
1	BAY LEAF		
3	OR 4 FRESH THYME SPRIGS		
1 1/2	TEASPOONS SALT		

The chard and duck confit infuse this lentil soup with an array of rich, complex flavors that belie the simplicity of the preparation. I like to fix the soup for a crowd and serve it with a salad of greens and citrus fruit plus a hearty red wine to make a satisfying meal. Look for duck confit at meat markets or specialty gourmet shops. The dark meat of roasted turkey leg or thigh could be substituted. Spinach or kale can replace the chard, but add the kale at the same time as the lentils. Stir in the spinach during the last 5 minutes of cooking.

Using a sharp knife, cut along the edges of the wide midrib of the chard leaves and remove them. Mince the ribs. Roll the leaves lengthwise into a tight roll and cut crosswise into 1/4-inch pieces. Set the ribs and leaves aside.

In a large, heavy-bottomed saucepan or soup pot over medium heat, heat the 2 teaspoons olive oil. Add the onion and sauté until just translucent, 3 to 4 minutes. Add the garlic and carrot and sauté for 2 to 3 minutes, then stir in the lentils and water. Bring to a boil, then reduce the heat to low. Add the bay leaf, thyme, 1 teaspoon of the salt, and the pepper and cook for

about 15 minutes. Add the chard ribs, leaves, and the duck legs. Cook until the lentils are almost tender, 20 to 25 minutes longer.

Transfer the duck legs to a cutting board, remove the skin, and discard it. Cut off the meat, coarsely chop it, and stir it into the soup. Cook until the lentils are tender but not mushy, about 10 minutes longer. Remove the thyme and bay leaf and discard. Add the remaining 1/2 teaspoon salt.

Meanwhile, in a large skillet over medium-high heat, heat the 1/4 cup olive oil. Add 4 baguette slices and fry until golden, about 3 minutes. Turn and fry the other side until golden, about 2 minutes. Transfer to paper towels to drain. Repeat with the remaining 4 baguette slices.

Ladle the soup into soup bowls and garnish each with a fried crouton.

tortilla soup with green garnish

tortilla strips

1/4	CUP CORN OIL, EXTRA-VIRGIN OLIVE OIL OR OTHER VEGETABLE OIL
4	TO 6 CORN TORTILLAS, HALVED AND CUT INTO 1/2-INCH-WIDE STRIPS
1/2	TO 1 TEASPOON SALT

soup

2	TABLESPOONS, PLUS 2 TEASPOONS EXTRA-VIRGIN OLIVE OIL OR CORN OIL
1/2	MEDIUM YELLOW ONION, SLICED FROM TOP TO BOTTOM INTO THIN SLIVERS
2	TO 3 CLOVES GARLIC, MINCED
2	TOMATOES, DICED
3/4	TEASPOON SALT
11/4	TEASPOONS DRIED OREGANO
6	CUPS CHICKEN BROTH
1	SKINLESS, BONELESS CHICKEN BREAST HALF, ABOUT 12 OUNCES
1/4	TEASPOON FRESHLY GROUND PEPPER

This is comfort food at its best. A soothing broth, spiked with just enough heat to warm you clear through, topped with a generous stack of finely shredded cabbage and sprigs of mâche, plus traditional garnishes of cilantro, avocado, dried chiles, and, of course, freshly made tortilla strips. Pan-seared chicken breast is added toward the end to transform the soup into a hearty one-dish meal. However, if you prefer a vegetarian version, omit the chicken and use vegetable broth instead of chicken broth. Make extra tortillas strips if you plan on nibbling while you cook. Julienned spinach can be substituted for the mâche.

To make the tortilla strips: In a large, heavy-bottomed saucepan over medium-high heat, heat the oil. Add the tortilla strips a few at a time and fry until lightly golden, about 2 minutes. Using a slotted spoon, transfer to paper towels to drain. Sprinkle with a little salt. Set aside.

To make the soup: In a large saucepan over medium-high heat, heat the 2 tablespoons oil. Add the onion and sauté until barely translucent, 1 to 2 minutes. Add the garlic and sauté for 1 minute. Stir in the tomatoes, 1/2 teaspoon of the salt, and 1 teaspoon of the oregano. Add the chicken broth, reduce the heat to low, and simmer until the tomatoes have melted into the broth and the onion is very soft, about 30 minutes.

While the soup is simmering, season the chicken breast half with the remaining 1/4 teaspoon salt, the remaining 1/4 teaspoon oregano, and the pepper. In a small skillet over medium-high heat, heat the 2 teaspoons oil. Add the chicken and sear until golden, about 3 minutes. Turn and sear the other side for about 3 minutes. Reduce the heat to low and cook the chicken for 1 minute longer on each side. Transfer to a cutting board and cut into 1/2-inch pieces. The chicken will still be pink on the inside, but it will finish cooking in the broth. When the soup is almost done, add the chicken and cook for 3 to 4 minutes.

Meanwhile, prepare the garnishes: Heat a dry small skillet over medium-high heat. Toast the chiles, using the back of a wooden

2 LARGE DRIED RED CHILES, SUCH AS ANAHEIM,
   CALIFORNIA, OR ANCHO

2 TABLESPOONS FRESH CILANTRO LEAVES

1 RIPE AVOCADO, PEELED, PITTED, AND CUT
   INTO ¼-INCH CUBES

¼ SMALL HEAD GREEN CABBAGE, THINLY SLICED
   AND CUT INTO 1-INCH-LONG PIECES

1 CUP MÂCHE OR CHOPPED STEMMED SPINACH

spoon or a spatula to push them against the bottom of the skillet, until soft and aromatic, 1 to 2 minutes. Turn and toast the other side for 1 to 2 minutes. Transfer the chiles to a cutting board, remove the stems and seeds, and discard. Chop the chiles into small pieces and set aside.

Ladle the soup into soup bowls and garnish as follows: Stir an equal amount of the cilantro into each bowl, then arrange the tortilla strips around the inside edges of the bowls, followed by the avocado and a sprinkling of the dried chiles, depending upon taste. Pile a generous tablespoon of the cabbage into the center of each bowl, and top with 3 sprigs of mâche. Serve immediately.

GREENS AND SALADS ARE VIRTUALLY SYNONYMOUS. TAKE SOME LETTUCE, MÂCHE, CABBAGE, RADICCHIO, WATERCRESS, ARUGULA— JUST ABOUT ANY GREEN YOU CAN THINK OF—THEN TOSS WITH A VINAIGRETTE OR CREAMY DRESSING, AND YOU'VE CREATED A SALAD.

A simple green salad can also serve as the base for additional ingredients, many of them found in a well-stocked pantry or refrigerator. You might toss in nuts, cheeses, olives, or cured meats or fish, such as bacon, prosciutto, or smoked salmon. Other possibilities include croutons, beans, eggs, or vegetables, such as beets, tomatoes, carrots, peppers, or potatoes. Fish, shellfish, poultry, and meats can be added as well to transform the salad into a main dish. Depending upon your choice of ingredients, your salad may take an Asian turn, reflect the fiery flavors of Mexico, or boast the sun-drenched tastes of the Mediterranean. Salads offer endless variations, and are quick and easy to make. OPPOSITE PAGE: Frisée, Mâche, and Pear Salad with Toasted Pecans (page 77)

belgian endive, carrot, and cilantro salad
with sesame vinaigrette

¼   CUP RICE WINE VINEGAR

½   TEASPOON SESAME OIL

¼   TEASPOON SALT

¼   TEASPOON FRESHLY GROUND PEPPER

5   HEADS BELGIAN ENDIVE

1   CARROT, PEELED AND GRATED

1   CUP FRESH CILANTRO LEAVES

This light, refreshing salad reflects the flavors of East and West. Napa cabbage can be substituted for the Belgian endive, and mint and parsley tossed in with the cilantro.

In a large salad bowl, combine the vinegar, oil, salt, and pepper and mix well with a fork. Using a small, sharp knife, cut an inverted V in the base of each Belgian endive to remove the core. Julienne the heads lengthwise and put them in the bowl. Add the carrot and cilantro, toss to coat well with the vinaigrette, and serve.

radicchio and parsley salad with lemon-garlic vinaigrette

1/4 TO 1/2 TEASPOON COARSE SEA SALT

1 CLOVE GARLIC, COARSELY CHOPPED

2/3 CUP EXTRA-VIRGIN OLIVE OIL

1/2 TEASPOON FRESHLY GROUND PEPPER

1 TO 1 1/2 TABLESPOONS FRESH LEMON JUICE

3 CUPS TORN RADICCHIO LEAVES

1 CUP FRESH FLAT-LEAF PARSLEY LEAVES

This is a classic salad in Chioggia, Italy, where aficionados of the slightly bitter, brilliantly colored radicchio find it the perfect prelude to fresh fish from the city's bustling port. Sometimes individual salad bowls are brought to the table along with a big bowl of torn radicchio and parsley leaves, a cruet or bottle of olive oil, lemon halves, garlic cloves, salt, and pepper. You mix the vinaigrette in your bowl to your own liking, then add the radicchio and parsley. I find it a very appealing custom. The sharp edges of the sea salt crystals help cut the garlic, producing a thick paste to incorporate into the vinaigrette. If radicchio on its own seems too austere, try tossing it with romaine and watercress or perhaps Belgian endive. Offer plenty of crusty bread with this salad.

In a large salad bowl, combine 1/4 teaspoon of the salt and the garlic and crush them together with a fork to form a paste. Add the olive oil and blend with the fork. Add the pepper and 1 tablespoon of the lemon juice, and continue to blend. Taste. The vinaigrette should taste of the unctuous olive oil and salt, with an underlying bite of garlic, pepper, and lemon. Add more salt or lemon juice if desired. Add the radicchio and parsley and toss the leaves over and over to coat very well with the vinaigrette. They should be glistening. Divide equally among 4 salad plates.

mâche, prosciutto, and parsnip chip salad

2   PARSNIPS

1/3 CUP EXTRA-VIRGIN OLIVE OIL

1 1/2 TABLESPOONS SHERRY VINEGAR

1/4 TEASPOON SALT, PLUS MORE AS NEEDED

1/2 TEASPOON COARSELY GROUND WHITE PEPPER

4   CUPS MÂCHE

4   OUNCES THINLY SLICED PROSCIUTTO, SLIVERED

A fluffy stack of tender mâche laced with slivers of prosciutto contrasts in flavor and texture to deep-fried sweet parsnip slices, which are crunchy on the outside, soft on the inside. Other tender greens, such as arugula, watercress, baby spinach, or mesclun, can be substituted for the mâche.

Peel the parsnips and cut them crosswise into 1 1/2-inch pieces. Slice each piece lengthwise into 1/4-inch-thick pieces. Stack a few together and trim off the edges to make squares. Repeat with the remaining pieces. Set aside.

In a large salad bowl, combine half of the olive oil, the vinegar, the 1/4 teaspoon salt, and the white pepper and mix well with a fork. Taste and add more salt if desired. Add the mâche and prosciutto and toss to coat well with the dressing and distribute the prosciutto. Divide equally among 4 salad plates.

In a medium saucepan over medium-high heat, heat the remaining oil. Add the parsnips a few at a time (do not overcrowd the pan) and fry until golden, about 1 minute. Turn and fry the other side, about 1 minute. Transfer to paper towels to drain briefly.

Divide the hot chips among the salads, tucking some of the chips into the greens. Serve immediately.

frisée, mâche, and pear salad with toasted pecans

SERVES 4

1	FIRM YET RIPE PEAR, SUCH AS BOSC OR RED BARTLETT	1/4	TEASPOON GROUND CARDAMOM
2	TABLESPOONS FRESH LEMON JUICE MIXED WITH 1 TEASPOON SUGAR	2	CUPS TORN FRISÉE, PALE INNER LEAVES ONLY
1/3	CUP PECANS	2	CUPS MÂCHE
1/4	CUP EXTRA-VIRGIN OLIVE OIL		
2	TABLESPOONS RED WINE VINEGAR		
2	TEASPOONS BALSAMIC VINEGAR		
1/4	TEASPOON SALT		
1/2	TEASPOON FRESHLY GROUND PEPPER		

Lacy sprigs of ivory frisée and clusters of brilliant-green mâche create a visually inviting background and offer a contrast in tastes. Here the greens are garnished with seasonal fruit and nuts, but you could take a savory approach by topping the greens with deep-fried oysters and garlic croutons, or slivers of roasted duck breast and a crumble of feta cheese. Small romaine leaves or mesclun mix might be used instead of the frisée and mâche.

Peel the pear, cut it in half lengthwise, and remove the seeds and core. Use a metal teaspoon to scoop out the seeds and the fibers surrounding them, and then run the tip of the spoon along the core to remove those fibers. Cut each half in half again, then slice each quarter into 1/4-inch-thick slices, keeping the slices attached at the narrow end of the pear. Using a spatula and keeping the slices together, transfer the pear to a plate. Fan out the slices slightly, then drizzle with the lemon juice mixture.

In a dry small skillet over medium heat, toast the pecans, stirring occasionally, until they are fragrant and beginning to brown slightly, about 4 minutes. Remove from the heat, let cool, and chop coarsely. Set aside.

In a large salad bowl, combine the olive oil, red wine vinegar, and balsamic vinegar and mix well with a fork. Add the salt, pepper, and cardamom and mix. Add the frisée and mâche and toss to coat well with the dressing.

Divide the greens equally among 4 salad plates, and top each with a fan of quartered pear and some of the pecans.

green herb and mâche salad with sherry-shallot vinaigrette

¼ CUP EXTRA-VIRGIN OLIVE OIL

2 TABLESPOONS MINCED SHALLOT

2 TABLESPOONS SHERRY VINEGAR

¼ TEASPOON SALT, PLUS MORE AS NEEDED

¼ TEASPOON FRESHLY GROUND PEPPER

½ CUP FRESH FLAT-LEAF PARSLEY LEAVES

¼ CUP MINCED FRESH CHIVES

¼ CUP FRESH CILANTRO LEAVES

3 CUPS MÂCHE

Bright, crisp flavors of fresh herbs play against the background notes of deep-green mâche. You can vary the herbs according to your taste. If you'd like, substitute arugula, spinach, or mesclun for the mâche, and add a favorite lettuce as well. This salad is particularly good paired with a cheese course, or served as an accompaniment to roasted duck, pork, or chicken.

In large salad bowl, combine the olive oil, shallot, vinegar, the ¼ teaspoon salt, and the pepper and mix well with a fork. Taste and add more salt if desired. Add the parsley, chives, cilantro, and mâche and toss to coat well with the dressing. Divide the greens equally among 4 salad plates.

classic caesar salad

1/2	CUP EXTRA-VIRGIN OLIVE OIL		2	HEARTS OF ROMAINE LETTUCE, LEAVES SEPARATED
2	CUPS STALE BREAD CUBES, WITH CRUSTS, PREFERABLY FROM A BAGUETTE OR STURDY COUNTRY BREAD		1	EGG
1/2	TEASPOON COARSE SEA SALT		1	ONE-OUNCE CHUNK PARMESAN CHEESE
3	CLOVES GARLIC			
4	ANCHOVY FILLETS, COARSELY CHOPPED, PLUS 4 WHOLE FILLETS FOR GARNISHING			
1	TEASPOON WORCESTERSHIRE SAUCE			
2	TABLESPOONS RED WINE VINEGAR			
1/2	TEASPOON FRESHLY GROUND PEPPER			

Hearts of romaine are the essential green for this salad, which purportedly was invented in the 1920s in Tijuana, Mexico. Today, some version of Caesar salad appears on the menus of both down-home and white-tablecloth restaurants across the country, as well as in ready-to-use salad kits sold in supermarkets. It is an easy salad to make, and a well-stocked pantry should have all the ingredients at hand. You will only need to buy the romaine hearts. The classic Caesar does contain raw egg, which you can omit if you wish. I love using homemade croutons. They can be prepared ahead and stored in an airtight container at room temperature for up to a week. Sea salt is recommended because its crystals have sharp edges that cut into the garlic, creating a smooth paste that forms the base for the dressing.

To make the croutons: In a large skillet over medium-high heat, heat 1/4 cup of the olive oil. Add the bread cubes and fry, turning as needed, until golden on all sides, about 5 minutes. Transfer to paper towels to drain. Set aside.

In a large salad bowl, combine the salt and garlic and crush them together with a fork to form a paste. Add the chopped anchovies and crush them into the paste. Whisk in the Worcestershire sauce, vinegar, and pepper. Drizzle in the remaining 1/4 cup olive oil, whisking to make a thick dressing.

Add the romaine and three fourths of the croutons to the bowl. Toss the leaves and croutons gently to coat well with the dressing. Crack the egg over the leaves, break the yolk, and toss the salad again to incorporate the egg. Top the salad with the remaining croutons. Using a vegetable peeler or a paring knife, scrape the cheese to make shavings and scatter the cheese over the salad. Garnish with the whole anchovy fillets. Serve immediately.

romaine, parsley, and celery salad with shaved parmesan SERVES 4

1/4 CUP EXTRA-VIRGIN OLIVE OIL

1 TABLESPOON RED WINE VINEGAR

1/2 TEASPOON COARSE SEA SALT

1/2 TEASPOON FRESHLY GROUND PEPPER

8 TO 10 CELERY STALKS

12 TO 14 ROMAINE LETTUCE LEAVES,
TORN INTO BITE-SIZED PIECES

1/2 CUP FRESH FLAT-LEAF PARSLEY LEAVES

1 2½-OUNCE CHUNK PARMESAN CHEESE

With its fine crunch and hearty flavor, romaine provides the perfect backdrop for a salad that includes lots of intense Parmesan cheese. Celery, which is intriguingly fresh yet pungent, is often overlooked as a salad ingredient. Here, it adds further depth to this simple salad, which I like to serve alongside roast chicken, lasagna, pork chops, or braised short ribs. Mesclun, spinach, arugula, or watercress can be substituted for the romaine.

In a large salad bowl, combine the olive oil and vinegar and mix well with a fork. Stir in the salt and pepper. Set aside.

To remove the strings from the celery, turn the rounded side of the stalk toward you and, using a paring knife, pull the strings toward you and down. Using a chef's knife or a mandoline, cut the celery crosswise into the thinnest possible slices. Add the celery to the salad bowl and toss to coat well with the dressing. Using a slotted spoon, transfer the celery to another bowl.

Add the romaine and parsley to the salad bowl and toss to coat well with the dressing. Pile the greens high on a platter and top with the celery. Using a vegetable peeler or a paring knife, scrape the cheese to make thin sheets and layer them over the celery.

beet and mesclun salad with blood oranges and goat cheese SERVES 4

12 BABY RED, YELLOW, OR STRIPED CHIOGGIA BEETS,
   OR 3 MEDIUM RED OR YELLOW BEETS,
   OR A COMBINATION

3 TABLESPOONS EXTRA-VIRGIN OLIVE OIL

2/3 CUP FRESH BLOOD ORANGE JUICE

1/4 CUP SHERRY VINEGAR

1/2 SCANT TEASPOON SALT

1/2 SCANT TEASPOON FRESHLY GROUND PEPPER

4 CUPS MESCLUN OR MIXED BABY LETTUCES

2 BLOOD ORANGES, PEELED, CUT INTO 1/2-INCH-THICK
   SLICES, AND SEEDED

3 OUNCES SOFT GOAT CHEESE, CRUMBLED

2 TABLESPOONS MINCED FRESH BASIL

4 TABLESPOONS ALMONDS, TOASTED AND CHOPPED

3 TABLESPOONS GRATED BLOOD ORANGE ZEST

Beets and oranges are a classic combination, and serving them on a bed of mesclun shows off their color and flavors. The hint of raspberry flavor in the blood oranges and their deep garnet hue add extra dimensions, although navel oranges could be used instead. You could also compose your own mesclun mix, tossing together different greens and lettuces, such as arugula, radicchio, and romaine, or iceberg, romaine, and watercress.

Preheat oven to 350 degrees F.

Cut the greens from the beets, leaving about 1/2 inch of the stems attached. Reserve the greens for another use. Rub the beets with 1 tablespoon of the olive oil, put them in a baking dish, and roast until tender when pierced with a fork, about 30 minutes for baby beets and about 1 hour and 15 minutes for medium ones. Let stand until cool enough to handle, about 10 minutes. Slip the skins off the beets, rinse, and dry. Cut the beets into 1/4-inch-thick slices and put them in a medium bowl.

In a small saucepan over high heat, combine the orange juice, vinegar, salt, and pepper and bring to a boil. Reduce the heat to medium and cook until the liquid is reduced to about 1/2 cup, about 10 minutes. Remove from the heat and let cool for about 10 minutes. Add the remaining 2 tablespoons olive oil and mix with a fork. Pour about half of the vinaigrette over the beets and stir them gently to coat.

Divide the mesclun equally among 4 salad plates. Using a slotted spoon, remove the beets from the bowl and arrange slices of beets, alternating with the orange slices, on the mesclun. Combine the remaining vinaigrette with the accumulated juices in the bowl and pour over the salads. Top the salads with the goat cheese and a sprinkling of the basil. Scatter the almonds and orange zest over all.

iceberg wedges with blue cheese dressing

3	OUNCES BLUE CHEESE, SUCH AS POINT REYES BLUE, MAYTAG, OR BLEU D'AUVERGNE	6	RED CHERRY TOMATOES FOR GARNISHING (OPTIONAL)
1/2	CUP HOMEMADE OR PURCHASED MAYONNAISE	6	YELLOW CHERRY TOMATOES FOR GARNISHING (OPTIONAL)
2	TABLESPOONS EXTRA-VIRGIN OLIVE OIL		
3	TO 6 TABLESPOONS HALF-AND-HALF OR MILK		
1	TABLESPOON WHITE WINE OR CHAMPAGNE VINEGAR		
1/2	TEASPOON FRESHLY GROUND PEPPER		
4	WEDGES OF ICEBERG LETTUCE, EACH ABOUT 1 1/2 INCHES THICK		
2	TABLESPOONS MINCED FRESH CHIVES		

An American salad favorite from the 1950s, the iceberg wedge is making a comeback. Crunchy and crisp, the lettuce is a delicious base for a generous drizzling of homemade blue cheese dressing. Thousand Island or ranch-style dressing would be equally good choices. I like to serve this salad as an accompaniment to a classic main course, such as steak and baked potatoes.

In a small bowl, mash the cheese with a fork, then add the mayonnaise and olive oil. Mix with the fork, blending the ingredients together. Add 3 tablespoons of the half-and-half and the vinegar and stir. The dressing should be thick but nearly pourable, with lumps of cheese in it. If it is too thick, add a little more half-and-half. Stir in the pepper.

Place a wedge of lettuce on each of 4 salad plates and drizzle the dressing equally over the lettuce. Sprinkle with the chives and garnish with the red and yellow cherry tomatoes if desired.

mâche salad with figs, hazelnuts, and goat cheese

- 3 TABLESPOONS, PLUS 1 TEASPOON HAZELNUT OIL, WALNUT OIL, OR EXTRA-VIRGIN OLIVE OIL
- 1½ TO 2 TEASPOONS RASPBERRY VINEGAR
- ½ TEASPOON SALT
- ½ TEASPOON FRESHLY GROUND PEPPER
- 4 CUPS MÂCHE
- 6 SOFT, RIPE FIGS, HALVED LENGTHWISE
- ½ TEASPOON BALSAMIC VINEGAR
- 2 TABLESPOONS WATER
- 2 TABLESPOONS CHOPPED HAZELNUTS, TOASTED
- 2 TO 3 OUNCES SOFT GOAT CHEESE

The warm, sweet figs bring out the nutty taste of the mâche, which is complemented by the nuts and the nut oil in the dressing. In winter, when fresh figs aren't available, you can substitute pears or apples. If you prefer a salad with sharper flavors, use arugula and watercress plus a little radicchio. Or, try baby spinach leaves or mesclun.

In a large salad bowl, combine the 3 tablespoons oil, 1½ teaspoons of the raspberry vinegar, the salt, and pepper and mix well with a fork. Taste and add the remaining ½ teaspoon raspberry vinegar if desired. Add the mâche and toss to coat well with the dressing. Divide the mâche equally among 4 salad plates.

In a nonstick skillet over medium-high heat, heat the 1 teaspoon oil. Add the figs, cut-side down, and cook until they are warmed through and beginning to caramelize, about 2 minutes.

Using a spatula, gently place 3 fig halves, cut-side up, on each salad. Set the skillet over high heat, add the balsamic vinegar and water, and stir to scrape up any bits that cling to the bottom of the pan. Cook until the liquid is reduced to a generous 1 tablespoon, about 30 seconds. Drizzle the liquid over the figs. Scatter the hazelnuts over the top and garnish each with a spoonful of the goat cheese.

warm escarole and frisée salad with bacon and potatoes

6 SMALL YUKON GOLD OR RED POTATOES,
   ABOUT 1¾ POUNDS TOTAL

1½ TEASPOONS SALT

6 THICK-CUT BACON SLICES, CUT INTO ½-INCH PIECES

1 TABLESPOON WHITE WINE OR CHAMPAGNE VINEGAR

2½ TABLESPOONS EXTRA-VIRGIN OLIVE OIL

½ TEASPOON DIJON MUSTARD

1 TEASPOON MINCED SHALLOT

1 TABLESPOON MINCED FRESH TARRAGON

2 CUPS TORN FRISÉE, PALE INNER LEAVES ONLY

2 CUPS TORN ESCAROLE LEAVES,
   PALE INNER LEAVES ONLY

Escarole and frisée are sturdy greens that can stand up to heat and assertive dressings as well as rustic ingredients, such as the bacon and potatoes in this salad. With the addition of a handful or two of Gruyère cheese cubes and some homemade croutons, this can become a main-course salad—and it is one of my favorites. Radicchio and romaine or mesclun might be substituted for the escarole and frisée.

Put the potatoes in a medium saucepan and add water to cover by 2 inches. Add 1 teaspoon of the salt and bring to a boil over high heat. Reduce the heat to medium-low, cover, and cook until the potatoes are just tender when pierced with a fork, 15 to 20 minutes. Drain the potatoes and let stand until cool enough to handle, about 10 minutes.

Meanwhile, in a medium skillet over medium-high heat, fry the bacon until golden, about 5 minutes. Turn and fry until the other side is golden, about 3 minutes. Transfer to paper towels to drain. Pour off all but 1 tablespoon of the fat, reserving it in the skillet.

Reduce the heat to medium-low, add the vinegar to the skillet, and heat gently for 1 to 2 minutes, stirring to scrape up any bits that cling to the bottom of the pan. Pour the mixture into a large salad bowl. Add the olive oil and the remaining ½ teaspoon salt, blending them into the fat and vinegar with a fork. Blend in the mustard, shallot, and tarragon. Set aside.

Peel the still-warm potatoes and cut them into ½-inch cubes. Add them to the salad bowl and stir gently to coat with the dressing. Using a slotted spoon, transfer them to another bowl. Add the frisée and escarole to the salad bowl and toss to coat well with the dressing.

Divide the greens equally among 4 salad plates, top with equal portions of the potatoes, and garnish with the bacon.

layered salad with beefsteak tomatoes, romaine, arugula, and bacon

12 BACON SLICES

12 TO 16 ROMAINE LETTUCE LEAVES, LIGHT GREEN INNER LEAVES ONLY

1/4 CUP EXTRA-VIRGIN OLIVE OIL

1½ TABLESPOONS RED WINE VINEGAR

1 TEASPOON BALSAMIC VINEGAR

1 TEASPOON SALT

1 TEASPOON FRESHLY GROUND PEPPER

2 CUPS BABY ARUGULA LEAVES

4 BEEFSTEAK TOMATOES, CUT INTO ½-INCH-THICK SLICES

2 OUNCES BLUE CHEESE, SUCH AS MAYTAG, BLEU D'AUVERGNE, OR STILTON, CRUMBLED (OPTIONAL)

If you enjoy bacon, lettuce, and tomato sandwiches as much as I do, you will love this salad. You can serve it with toasted slices of baguette or another favorite bread. Mâche is an excellent substitute for the arugula, and watercress or spinach could be used as well.

Preheat the broiler.

Put the bacon on a broiler pan and broil about 4 inches from the heat until lightly browned, 3 to 4 minutes. Turn and broil on the other side for 2 to 3 minutes. Transfer to paper towels to drain. Alternatively, fry in a large skillet over medium-high heat, turning once, until crisp, about 7 minutes.

Arrange 3 or 4 romaine leaves, curved-side up, on each of 4 salad plates. In a small bowl, combine the olive oil, red wine vinegar, balsamic vinegar, and 1/2 teaspoon each of the salt and pepper and mix well with a fork. Drizzle about half of the vinaigrette over the romaine leaves. Scatter equal amounts of the arugula over the romaine and drizzle with the remaining vinaigrette. Arrange the tomatoes on the greens, and season with the remaining 1/2 teaspoon salt and pepper. Top each salad with 3 bacon slices. Garnish with the cheese if desired.

taco salad with cabbage and red snapper

red snapper

1	TABLESPOON CORN OIL
1 1/2	POUNDS RED SNAPPER
1	TABLESPOON EXTRA-VIRGIN OLIVE OIL
3/4	TEASPOON SALT
1/2	TEASPOON FRESHLY GROUND BLACK PEPPER
1	TEASPOON CALIFORNIA OR OTHER MILD CHILI POWDER
1/8	TEASPOON CAYENNE PEPPER
1	TEASPOON CRUSHED DRIED OREGANO

salsa

3	CUPS WATER
5	TOMATILLOS
3	HUNGARIAN WAX CHILES OR GREEN CALIFORNIA CHILES, SEEDED AND CHOPPED
2	SERRANO CHILES, SEEDED AND CHOPPED
2	TABLESPOONS CHOPPED YELLOW ONION
1	CLOVE GARLIC, MINCED
1/4	CUP CHOPPED FRESH CILANTRO
1	RIPE AVOCADO, PEELED AND PITTED

In Mexican cooking, crisp tortillas are used much like dry bread is in France and Italy—as an addition to salads, soups, eggs, and cheese dishes to soak up sauces as well as lend texture and character. I find that frying up my own tortillas produces a fresher, better ingredient than using purchased taco shells or chips. It only takes a few minutes and is well worth the effort. Virtually any combination of greens will be delicious in this salad, but I especially like the crunch of the cabbage. Grilled beef or chicken can stand in for the red snapper.

To prepare the red snapper: Oil a baking dish with the corn oil. Rub the fish all over with the olive oil. In a small bowl, mix together the salt, black pepper, chili powder, cayenne, and oregano. Rub the fish all over with the seasoning mixture. Put the fish in the prepared baking dish, cover with plastic wrap, and refrigerate for 1 hour.

To make the salsa: In a medium saucepan over medium heat, bring the water to a boil. Add the tomatillos, papery husks and all, and cook for 5 minutes. Drain. When the tomatillos are cool enough to handle, remove the papery husks and discard. Finely chop the tomatillos and put in a small bowl. Add the Hungarian and serrano chiles, onion, garlic, and cilantro and stir to mix. Add the avocado, mashing it into the other ingredients with a fork. The salsa should be chunky rather than smooth. Set aside.

To make the salad: If you are frying tortillas, in a large saucepan or skillet over medium-high heat, heat the corn oil. Add the tortilla triangles a few at a time and fry until golden, about 1 minute on each side. Using tongs, transfer to paper towels to drain. Set aside.

Preheat the oven to 450 degrees F.

Remove the plastic wrap from the fish. Bake until the fish is just opaque and flakes easily with a fork, 10 to 12 minutes. Set aside.

Put the red and green cabbage in a large salad bowl, add the lime juice, and toss. Add the salt and chili powder and toss again. Add the tomatoes and the 3/4 cup *crema* and toss again. Set aside 8 tortilla chips for garnishing. Using your hands,

salad

1/4	CUP CORN OIL, EXTRA-VIRGIN OLIVE OIL, OR OTHER VEGETABLE OIL
5	CORN TORTILLAS, EACH CUT INTO 8 TRIANGLES, OR 3 TO 4 CUPS PURCHASED TORTILLA CHIPS
1½	CUPS THINLY SLICED RED CABBAGE
1	CUP THINLY SLICED GREEN CABBAGE
½	CUP FRESH LIME JUICE
¾	TEASPOON SALT
1	TEASPOON CALIFORNIA OR OTHER MILD CHILI POWDER
2	TOMATOES, CHOPPED
¾	CUP, PLUS 2 TABLESPOONS *CREMA* (MEXICAN CREAM), CRÈME FRAÎCHE, OR HEAVY CREAM WITH 2 TABLESPOONS BUTTERMILK ADDED
½	CUP FRESH CILANTRO LEAVES

break the remaining ones into several pieces. Add the chips and cilantro to the cabbage and toss. Divide equally among 4 dinner plates. Break the fish into about 12 pieces and put equal amounts on each salad. Top each with some of the 2 tablespoons *crema* and a healthy portion of the salsa. Garnish with the reserved chips.

crab louis

1 CUP HOMEMADE OR PURCHASED MAYONNAISE

2 TABLESPOONS TO 1/4 CUP MILK, HALF-AND-HALF, OR HEAVY CREAM

1/4 CUP CHILI SAUCE OR KETCHUP

1/4 CUP MINCED GREEN ONIONS, WHITE PARTS ONLY

2 TABLESPOONS FRESH LEMON JUICE

2 TABLESPOONS MINCED SWEET PICKLE PLUS 1 TEASPOON PICKLE JUICE

1 TEASPOON WORCESTERSHIRE SAUCE

1/4 TEASPOON SALT, PLUS MORE AS NEEDED

1/2 TEASPOON FRESHLY GROUND PEPPER,

PLUS MORE AS NEEDED

4 TO 8 ICEBERG LETTUCE, ROMAINE, OR OTHER LETTUCE LEAVES

4 CUPS FINELY SHREDDED ROMAINE LETTUCE COMBINED WITH 1 CUP MÂCHE

3 CUPS FRESH LUMP CRABMEAT, PICKED OVER FOR SHELLS

2 HARD-BOILED EGGS, QUARTERED

Crab Louis is an American classic created by a hotel chef in Seattle at the end of the nineteenth century. Since then, crab Louis has become part of our seafood heritage, something we expect to find on the menus of good seafood restaurants. In its purest version, it is essentially a bed of lettuce leaves topped with thinly sliced or shredded lettuce, heaps of fresh crabmeat, and a mayonnaise-based dressing spiked with chili sauce. Then the salad is garnished with quarters of hard-boiled eggs. Like other traditional dishes, crab Louis has been interpreted in any number of ways, using different garnishes and lettuces and seasoning the dressing with various condiments. Iceberg or romaine lettuce as well as tender red or green leaf lettuce remain favorite greens, but mesclun can be used instead. Mâche mixed with romaine also makes a good combination. This version is relatively traditional.

In a small bowl, combine the mayonnaise and 2 tablespoons of the milk and mix with a fork until well blended. Stir in the chili sauce, green onions, lemon juice, pickles and pickle juice, and Worcestershire sauce and mix until well blended. Add the 1/4 teaspoon salt and 1/2 teaspoon pepper, taste, and add more if desired. For a thinner dressing, add a little more milk.

Line 4 salad plates or shallow bowls with the iceberg lettuce leaves. Divide the shredded romaine and mâche equally among the plates, then top each with one fourth of the crabmeat. Spoon the dressing equally over the salads and garnish with the hard-boiled eggs. Serve immediately.

greens with smoked trout and horseradish cream

1/4   CUP EXTRA-VIRGIN OLIVE OIL

2   TABLESPOONS TARRAGON OR CHAMPAGNE VINEGAR

2   TABLESPOONS MINCED SHALLOT

2   TABLESPOONS CHOPPED FRESH TARRAGON

1/2   TEASPOON SALT

1/2   TEASPOON FRESHLY GROUND WHITE PEPPER

2   CUPS MÂCHE

1   CUP STEMMED WATERCRESS LEAVES

1   CUP TORN FRISÉE, PALE INNER LEAVES ONLY

12   OUNCES SMOKED TROUT, BROKEN INTO
     BITE-SIZED PIECES

2   TABLESPOONS PURCHASED HORSERADISH CREAM

4   RED RADISHES, THINLY SLIVERED

This combination of greens—mâche, watercress, and frisée— provides a background of nutty, peppery, and slightly bitter flavors that are echoed in the horseradish cream. A mesclun mixture or a combination of shredded napa cabbage, arugula, and mâche might be used instead.

In a large salad bowl, combine the olive oil and vinegar and mix with a fork. Add the shallot, tarragon, salt, and white pepper and mix. Add the mâche, watercress, and frisée and toss to coat well with the dressing. Divide the greens equally among 4 salad plates. Top each with an equal portion of the smoked trout, tucking some of the trout into the greens. Drizzle with the horseradish cream and garnish with the radishes.

GREENS SHOW OFF THEIR VERSATILITY IN MAIN DISHES, APPEARING IN PASTAS, STUFF-INGS, AND BAKED CASSEROLES AS WELL AS BEING THE PRIMARY INGREDIENT IN GRATINS. THEY ARE EQUALLY AT HOME WITH FISH, POULTRY, AND MEATS AND ALSO WITH OTHER VEGETABLES.

In main dishes, greens are usually either cooked as the principal ingredient or added at the last minute, with just enough heat furnished to wilt them. Sturdy greens, such as kale, cabbage, chard, and the chicories, are especially suitable for main dishes because they stand up well to cooking, although tender greens can be used if given a light treatment. OPPOSITE PAGE: Chard Tart with Salmon and Bacon (page 102)

gratin of belgian endive with pancetta

---

4   OUNCES THINLY SLICED PANCETTA OR PROSCIUTTO,
    OR 8 BACON SLICES

8   MEDIUM HEADS BELGIAN ENDIVE

3   TABLESPOONS UNSALTED BUTTER

3   TABLESPOONS ALL-PURPOSE FLOUR

1/2 TEASPOON SALT, PLUS MORE AS NEEDED

1/4 TEASPOON FRESHLY GRATED NUTMEG

1/8 TEASPOON CAYENNE PEPPER

1   CUP MILK

1/4 CUP, PLUS 1 TABLESPOON FRESHLY
    GRATED GRUYÈRE CHEESE

1/2 TEASPOON FRESHLY GROUND BLACK PEPPER

The salty sweetness of air-cured pancetta and the rich, velvety smoothness of the béchamel sauce are perfect counterpoints to the slight bitterness of Belgian endive. This gratin is always a big hit when I serve it, even to people who have never tasted Belgian endive before. I often accompany it with a green salad, such as a classic Caesar (page 79) or simply romaine lettuce dressed with a vinaigrette, plus plenty of warm bread to soak up the sauce from the gratin.

In a medium skillet over medium heat, fry the pancetta or bacon until it is just barely crisp, about 3 minutes on each side. Transfer to paper towels to drain, then chop. If you are using prosciutto, do not cook it; simply chop it.

Preheat the oven to 350 degrees F. Butter the bottom and sides of a shallow ovenproof casserole that is just large enough to hold the Belgian endive.

Using a small, sharp knife, cut an inverted V in the base of each Belgian endive to remove the core. Set aside.

In a small, heavy-bottomed saucepan over medium heat, melt 2 tablespoons of the butter. When it foams, remove the pan from the heat and whisk in the flour, the 1/2 teaspoon salt, the nutmeg, and cayenne to form a paste. Return the pan to medium heat and add the milk in a slow, steady stream, whisking constantly. Reduce the heat to low and whisk until there are no lumps. Simmer, stirring occasionally, until the sauce is thick enough to coat the back of a spoon, about 15 minutes. Stir in the 1/4 cup cheese and the black pepper and cook, stirring, just until the cheese melts into the sauce, 2 to 3 minutes. Taste and add more salt if desired.

Arrange the endive in the prepared casserole and top with the pancetta, bacon, or prosciutto. Carefully pour the sauce over the top. Cut the remaining 1 tablespoon butter into small bits and dot the surface. Scatter the 1 tablespoon cheese over the top. Bake until a golden, bubbling crust forms and the endive is tender when pierced with a fork, 25 to 30 minutes. Using a spatula, remove the endive and serve hot.

savoy cabbage gratin

1   HEAD SAVOY CABBAGE, ABOUT 2 POUNDS

1   LARGE YELLOW ONION

4   TABLESPOONS UNSALTED BUTTER

1   TEASPOON SALT

1   TEASPOON FRESHLY GROUND PEPPER

1   TABLESPOON ALL-PURPOSE FLOUR

1   CUP MILK

2   TABLESPOONS FRESHLY GRATED GRUYÈRE CHEESE

2   TABLESPOONS FRESHLY GRATED PARMESAN CHEESE

3   TABLESPOONS HOMEMADE DRIED BREAD CRUMBS

Although this gratin makes a lovely side dish, I think it's hearty enough to serve as a main course, accompanied by a big green salad and slices of thick country bread. As the onions slowly cook in the butter, they release their sweetness. Then tender Savoy cabbage is added, creating an incredibly rich base for this dish and elevating what might otherwise be modest fare to centerpiece status. Green, red, or napa cabbage might be used instead, but I think the sweet flavor of Savoy cabbage marries perfectly with the onions.

Preheat the oven to 400 degrees F. Butter a large baking dish.

Using a sharp knife, quarter the cabbage lengthwise, cut out the solid core, and discard it. Cut the quarters lengthwise into very thin slices. Set aside.

Halve the onion lengthwise and, preferably using a mandoline, cut the onion into the thinnest possible slices. In a large, heavy-bottomed skillet with a tight-fitting lid over medium-high heat, melt 3 tablespoons of the butter. When it foams, add the onion, cover and reduce the heat to low. Let the onion sweat, stirring from time to time, until it is near dissolving but is not browned, 15 to 20 minutes. Add the cabbage. It might seem impossible to fit it in the pan, but the cabbage will cook down considerably. Cover the pan, even if the lid won't quite fit, and cook until the cabbage is wilted and will fit beneath the lid, 10 to 15 minutes. Uncover the pan and cook, stirring occasionally, until the cabbage is soft and translucent, 10 to 15 minutes longer.

Stir the salt and pepper into the cabbage mixture, then sprinkle the flour over the top and stir. Increase the heat to high and add the milk a little at a time, while stirring, to create a sauce. Continue cooking, stirring constantly, until the sauce is thickened, about 5 minutes. Spread the cabbage mixture evenly in the prepared baking dish.

In a small bowl, combine the Gruyère and Parmesan cheeses and the bread crumbs. Sprinkle over the cabbage mixture and dot with the remaining 1 tablespoon butter. Bake until the top is crusty and golden and the edges are bubbling, about 20 minutes. Spoon the gratin from the baking dish and serve hot.

shepherd's pie with three greens

6	MEDIUM RUSSET POTATOES, PEELED AND QUARTERED	1	TEASPOON FRESH THYME LEAVES
2 1/2	TEASPOONS SALT	1	TABLESPOON ALL-PURPOSE FLOUR
4	TABLESPOONS UNSALTED BUTTER	1 1/4	CUPS BEEF BROTH
1/3	CUP MILK	2	CUPS CHOPPED STEMMED SPINACH
1	EGG	1	CUP SHREDDED SAVOY OR GREEN CABBAGE
1	TEASPOON MINCED FRESH FLAT-LEAF PARSLEY	1	CUP CHOPPED KALE
1 1/2	TEASPOONS FRESHLY GROUND PEPPER		
2	POUNDS GROUND LEAN BEEF		
1/2	YELLOW ONION, MINCED		
2	FRESH BAY LEAVES OR 1 DRIED		

A classic English dish, shepherd's pie is essentially a beef or lamb stew that is topped with a creamy layer of mashed potatoes and then baked. This version includes a healthy component of greens along with the traditional meat and onions. To complete the meal, add a loaf of crusty bread and a salad, such as Belgian Endive, Carrot, and Cilantro Salad with Sesame Vinaigrette (page 74) or Green Herb and Mâche Salad with Sherry-Shallot Vinaigrette (page 78).

Put the potatoes in a large saucepan and add water to cover by 2 inches. Add 1 teaspoon of the salt and bring to a boil over high heat. Reduce the heat to medium and cook until the potatoes can be easily pierced with a fork but are not soggy, 25 to 30 minutes. Drain the potatoes, reserving about one fourth of the cooking water. Put the potatoes in a large bowl and mash them. While mashing, add 2 tablespoons of the butter, the reserved cooking water, the milk, egg, parsley, and 1/2 teaspoon each of the salt and pepper. Cover and set aside.

Preheat the oven to 375 degrees F.

In a large skillet over medium-high heat, melt 1 tablespoon of the butter. Break the ground beef into pieces, add to the skillet, and brown the beef, about 5 minutes. Add the onion, bay leaves, thyme, the remaining 1 teaspoon each of the salt and pepper, and the flour, stirring constantly. The flour will start to brown, which is what you want, because this will eventually give the stew its rich, dark color.

When the flour is nicely browned, after 3 to 4 minutes, add the beef broth a little at a time, stirring to scrape up any bits that cling to the bottom of the pan and gradually creating a sauce. Reduce the heat to low, add the spinach, cabbage, and kale, and cover the skillet. The greens will barely fit at first, but their volume will reduce considerably. Cook until the greens are thoroughly wilted, about 5 minutes. Remove the bay leaves and discard.

To assemble the dish, transfer the meat mixture to an ovenproof casserole large enough to hold all the ingredients. Spoon the potatoes evenly over the stew, covering it completely. Cut the remaining 1 tablespoon butter into bits and dot it over the top. Bake until the potatoes are lightly browned and the stew is bubbling, 15 to 20 minutes.

fettuccine with walnuts, arugula, and lemon

- 1/4 CUP EXTRA-VIRGIN OLIVE OIL
- 2 CLOVES GARLIC, MINCED
- 2/3 CUP (6 OUNCES) WALNUTS
- 1 1/2 TEASPOONS SALT
- 12 OUNCES FETTUCCINE
- 3 CUPS BABY ARUGULA LEAVES, STEMS INTACT, OR 1 BUNCH MATURE ARUGULA, STEMS AND MIDRIBS REMOVED, LEAVES COARSELY CHOPPED
- 2 TABLESPOONS CHICKEN BROTH
- 1 TEASPOON FRESHLY CRACKED PEPPER

- 2 TABLESPOONS LEMON ZEST
- 1/4 CUP FRESHLY GRATED PARMESAN CHEESE
- 2 TABLESPOONS FRESH LEMON JUICE
- 1 LEMON, CUT INTO 4 WEDGES

The acidity of the lemons accents the richness of the walnuts, while the arugula adds a little bite and color. For a slightly different version, you can substitute another tender green, such as mâche or baby spinach, for the arugula.

In a small skillet over medium heat, heat the olive oil. Add the garlic and sauté until lightly golden, about 3 minutes. Remove the pan from the heat and set aside.

In a dry medium skillet over medium heat, toast the walnuts, stirring occasionally, until they are lightly golden and fragrant, 4 to 5 minutes. Remove from the heat, let cool, and chop. Set aside.

In a pasta cooker or a large pot, bring 2 1/2 to 3 quarts of water to a boil over high heat. Add 1 teaspoon of the salt and the pasta. Return to a boil, then reduce the heat to medium and cook until the pasta is tender to the bite, 10 to 12 minutes. Drain immediately.

Put the arugula in the bottom of a large bowl and add the hot pasta. Add the chicken broth to the skillet with the garlic and heat over medium heat for 45 seconds to 1 minute, then pour it over the pasta, tossing to coat. Stir in the remaining 1/2 teaspoon salt, the pepper, lemon zest, half of the cheese, and all but about 1 tablespoon of the walnuts. Add the lemon juice and toss to combine. Garnish with the remaining cheese and walnuts, and serve with the lemon wedges.

chard tart with salmon and bacon

pastry

- 1¼ CUPS ALL-PURPOSE FLOUR
- ½ TEASPOON SALT
- ½ CUP (1 STICK) CHILLED UNSALTED BUTTER, CUT INTO SMALL PIECES
- ¼ CUP ICE WATER, PLUS 2 TABLESPOONS MORE IF NEEDED

filling

- 4 BACON SLICES
- 1 SALMON FILLET, ABOUT 4 OUNCES
- 1½ TEASPOONS SALT
- ½ TEASPOON FRESHLY GROUND BLACK PEPPER
- 2 TEASPOONS, PLUS 3 TABLESPOONS UNSALTED BUTTER
- ¼ CUP DRY WHITE WINE
- ¼ CUP WATER, PLUS MORE AS NEEDED
- 1 TABLESPOON FRESH LEMON JUICE

The flavor and color of the braised chard permeate this tart, while the salmon and bacon discreetly season the light custard. When served with a salad, the tart is perfect for brunch or a light supper. Spinach can be used instead of chard, but cook it for only 2 to 3 minutes. The pastry can be made the day before and refrigerated.

To make the pastry in a food processor: Combine the flour and salt. Add the butter and pulse until the mixture is crumbly, about 1 minute. With the machine running, dribble in the ¼ cup water until the dough forms a moist crumble and holds together when pinched, 2 to 3 minutes. If necessary, add more water a little at a time. Do not overprocess.

To the make the pastry by hand: Sift together the flour and salt in a bowl. Add the butter and, using a pastry blender or 2 knives, cut in the butter until pea-sized balls form. Add the water 1 tablespoon at a time, turning the dough lightly with a fork and then with your fingertips. Do not overwork the dough.

Lay a 16-inch-long sheet of plastic wrap on a work surface. Put the ball of dough on top of the plastic and top with another sheet of plastic the same size. Using your hands, pat and flatten the dough, then roll out the dough into an 8-inch round. Refrigerate for at least 1 hour or preferably overnight.

To make the filling: In a medium skillet over medium-high heat, fry the bacon until golden, about 5 minutes. Turn and fry until the other side is golden, about 3 minutes. Transfer to paper towels to drain.

Rub the salmon with about ¼ teaspoon of the salt and the black pepper. In a small skillet over medium-high heat, melt the 2 teaspoons butter. When it foams, add the salmon, skin-side down, and cook until the skin is slightly crisp, about 1 minute. Add the wine and cook for 30 to 45 seconds, stirring to scrape up any bits that cling to the bottom of the pan. Add the ¼ cup water and the lemon juice, cover, and reduce the heat to low. Cook, checking occasionally to make sure the liquid is not evaporating too quickly (add more water if necessary), until the fish is opaque and flakes easily with a fork, about 6 minutes. Transfer the salmon to a plate and set aside.

2   TABLESPOONS FINELY CHOPPED YELLOW ONION

6   CHARD LEAVES, CHOPPED (ABOUT 1 CUP)

3   EGGS

1   TEASPOON FRESH THYME LEAVES

2   CUPS HEAVY CREAM

1   TABLESPOON TOMATO PASTE

1/8 TEASPOON CAYENNE PEPPER

1/2 CUP (2 OUNCES) FRESHLY GRATED GRUYÈRE CHEESE

In a large skillet over medium-high heat, melt 1 tablespoon of the butter. When it foams, add the onion and sauté until translucent, 2 to 3 minutes. Add the chard, cover, and reduce the heat to medium-low. Cook until the chard is soft and wilted, about 3 minutes, then uncover the skillet. Stir the chard and continue to cook until it is soft and tender, 3 to 4 minutes longer. Drain off any juices and set aside.

Preheat the oven to 350 degrees F.

Remove the pastry from the refrigerator. Keeping the pastry between the sheets of plastic, roll it out into a 14-inch round, about 1/16 inch thick. Remove the top sheet of plastic, drape the pastry over the rolling pin, and unfold it over a 10-inch round quiche or tart pan, preferably with a removable bottom. Pat the dough into place, then trim off all but 1/2 inch of the excess. Fold the remaining dough under to make a slightly raised edge. Line the pastry with aluminum foil, add a layer of pie weights or dried beans, and bake until the edges of the pastry are pale gold and pull slightly away from the sides, about 15 minutes. Transfer the pan to a wire rack and remove the foil and weights.

In a medium bowl, combine the eggs, thyme, 1/2 teaspoon of the salt, the cream, tomato paste, and cayenne pepper and beat with an electric mixer or whisk by hand until blended. Stir in the chard mixture and the remaining 3/4 teaspoon salt. Remove the skin from the salmon, break the fish into smallish pieces, and stir it into the egg mixture. Crumble the bacon and stir into the mixture, then stir in 1/4 cup of the cheese. Pour the filling into the shell. Dot with the remaining 2 tablespoons butter and sprinkle with the remaining 1/4 cup cheese. Bake until the top is lightly browned and a knife inserted into the center of the tart comes out clean, 35 to 45 minutes.

Let cool for 10 to 15 minutes, then cut into wedges and serve hot or at room temperature.

fettuccine with baby bok choy, prosciutto, and pecans

1   TEASPOON SALT

12 OUNCES FRESH FETTUCCINE, PLAIN OR SPINACH

3   TABLESPOONS UNSALTED BUTTER,
    PLUS MORE AS NEEDED

1/4 TEASPOON FRESHLY GROUND PEPPER

1   TABLESPOON EXTRA-VIRGIN OLIVE OIL

4   GREEN-STEMMED BOK CHOY, CUT LENGTHWISE
    INTO 1/2-INCH-THICK SLICES

1/2 CUP (4 OUNCES) PECANS, COARSELY CHOPPED

4   OUNCES THINLY SLICED PROSCIUTTO, SLIVERED

The slightly sweet, peppery flavor of bok choy pairs well with the rich nuts and the cured meat in this pasta dish, which is bound together with butter and olive oil. For a more Italian version, replace the bok choy with chopped radicchio or escarole, and the pecans with walnuts or chestnuts.

Bring a large pot three fourths full of water to a boil over high heat. Add 3/4 teaspoon of the salt and the pasta and cook until tender, 3 to 4 minutes. Drain and transfer to a warmed serving platter. Fold in 1 tablespoon of the butter and the pepper. Cover loosely with aluminum foil.

In a large skillet over medium-high heat, melt the remaining 2 tablespoons butter with the olive oil. When the butter foams, add the bok choy and sauté until just wilted, about 3 minutes. Using a slotted spoon, transfer the bok choy to the pasta.

In the same skillet over medium-high heat, sauté the pecans and prosciutto until they are shiny, about 30 seconds, adding a little more butter if necessary. Fold the bok choy and half of the pecan mixture into the pasta. Taste and add more salt if desired. Garnish with the remaining pecan mixture and serve immediately.

escarole and lemon risotto

2   CUPS CHICKEN BROTH

2 3/4 CUPS WATER

3   TABLESPOONS UNSALTED BUTTER

2   TABLESPOONS EXTRA-VIRGIN OLIVE OIL

1   SHALLOT, MINCED

1 1/2 CUPS ARBORIO RICE

1/4 CUP FRESH LEMON JUICE

2   CUPS TORN ESCAROLE LEAVES,
     PALE INNER LEAVES ONLY

     ZEST OF 1 LEMON

1/3 CUP FRESHLY GRATED PARMESAN CHEESE

2   TABLESPOONS MINCED FRESH FLAT-LEAF PARSLEY

The pale-green escarole sweetens as it cooks, contributing flavor and texture to this delicate risotto. I like to serve it as a main course, but it's also delicious paired with sautéed fish, such as sole or trout. Frisée or radicchio can stand in for the escarole.

In a saucepan over medium-high heat, combine the chicken broth and water and bring to a simmer. Reduce the heat to low to maintain a simmer.

In a large heavy-bottomed saucepan over medium heat, melt 1 1/2 tablespoons of the butter with the olive oil. When the butter foams, reduce the heat to medium, add the shallot, and sauté until nearly transparent, 1 to 2 minutes. Add the rice and sauté, stirring, until the rice is glistening and is beginning to turn opaque, 2 to 3 minutes. Add 2 to 3 large ladlefuls of the simmering broth and cook, stirring often, until the broth is nearly absorbed, about 5 minutes. Add another 1/2 cup or so of broth and continue the process.

When the rice is nearly tender and about 3/4 cup of the broth is left, after about 15 minutes, add the lemon juice to the remaining broth, and add the escarole to the rice. Continue adding the broth to the rice, stirring often, until it is gone, the rice is tender, and the liquid is nearly absorbed, about 5 minutes longer.

Stir in the remaining 1 1/2 tablespoons butter, the lemon zest, cheese, and parsley. Serve immediately.

curried slaw with grilled halibut

1   TEASPOON GROUND TURMERIC

1   TEASPOON GROUND CORIANDER

1   TEASPOON GROUND CUMIN

1   TEASPOON SALT

1   TABLESPOON FRESH LEMON JUICE

2   TABLESPOONS HOMEMADE OR PURCHASED
    MAYONNAISE

4   CUPS GRATED GREEN CABBAGE

4   HALIBUT FILLETS, ABOUT 1 1/3 POUNDS TOTAL,
    EACH 3/4 TO 1 INCH THICK

2   TABLESPOONS EXTRA-VIRGIN OLIVE OIL

1/2   TEASPOON FRESHLY GROUND PEPPER

The spicy dressing on the slaw complements the slight mustardy flavor of the cabbage, creating a savory bed for grilled fish. Napa cabbage or a mixture of green and red cabbage can be used for the slaw, and any firm fish, such as shark, sea bass, or catfish, can stand in for the halibut.

In a large bowl, stir together the turmeric, coriander, cumin, 1/2 teaspoon of the salt, the lemon juice, and mayonnaise until well blended. Add the cabbage and toss to coat well with the dressing. Refrigerate for at least 30 minutes or up to 2 hours.

Meanwhile, prepare a hot charcoal or wood fire in a grill, heat a gas grill, or preheat a broiler. If using a grill, oil it well with olive oil or other vegetable oil.

Rub the halibut with the olive oil and season with the remaining 1/2 teaspoon salt and the pepper. Grill or broil the fish until it is firm to the touch and flakes easily with a fork, about 5 minutes on each side. To serve, mound the chilled slaw on 4 dinner plates, dividing evenly, and top each with a halibut fillet.

chicken, spinach, and apple sausage

MAKES 12 TO 15 PATTIES; SERVES 6 TO 8

1½ POUNDS SKINLESS, BONELESS CHICKEN BREASTS,
CUT INTO LARGE CHUNKS

4 OUNCES BACON

3 POUNDS SPINACH, STEMMED AND LEAVES
COARSELY CHOPPED

1 TABLESPOON UNSALTED BUTTER

2 GRANNY SMITH OR OTHER TART APPLES, PEELED,
CORED, GRATED, AND SQUEEZED DRY

2 TEASPOONS CORIANDER SEED

1 TEASPOON FENNEL SEED

2 TEASPOONS MIXED BLACK, WHITE, GREEN,
AND PINK PEPPERCORNS

1½ TEASPOONS SALT

½ TEASPOON FRESHLY GRATED NUTMEG

¼ TEASPOON CAYENNE PEPPER

3 TABLESPOONS OLIVE OIL

Spinach or other greens are often used in French sausage to add color, flavor, and moisture. In this version, grated apples add moisture as well. Lots of coriander and fennel plus nutmeg and cayenne impart a spicy kick. I like to serve the sausages with homemade applesauce and Sweet-and-Sour Red Cabbage (page 131) for a hearty meal. You don't need a meat grinder or sausage-stuffing equipment to make these sausages. A food processor grinds the meat, then the seasoned mixture is shaped into patties by hand. Of course, the mixture can be stuffed into casings instead. Cook and eat the sausages within one to two days of making them, or wrap in plastic wrap and freeze for up to three months.

Working in batches, put the chicken in a food processor and pulse a few times until coarsely ground. Transfer to a large bowl. Repeat with the bacon and add to the bowl with the chicken. Using your hands or a heavy wooden spoon, mix well.

Put the spinach in a large bowl of cold water. In a large skillet or sauté pan over medium-high heat, melt the butter. When it foams, remove the spinach from the water and, without drying it, add to the pan. Cover and cook until the spinach is thoroughly wilted but still bright green, 2 to 3 minutes. Drain the spinach in a colander but do not rinse it. Let stand until completely cool. Using the back of a wooden spoon, gently press the spinach against the sides of the colander to remove the excess liquid.

Add the spinach and the apples to the chicken mixture. In a small spice grinder or coffee grinder, or using a mortar and pestle, grind together the coriander, fennel, peppercorns, salt, and nutmeg until it is rather fine. Add to the chicken mixture along with the cayenne. Using your hands or a heavy wooden spoon, mix well to distribute all the ingredients. Shape the mixture into patties about 4 inches in diameter and 1/2 inch thick.

In a large skillet over medium-high heat, heat the olive oil. Add the sausage patties (you may need to do this in batches) and cook until browned, 3 to 4 minutes. Turn and cook the other side until browned, 3 to 4 minutes.

chicken breasts stuffed with arugula and capers

4   CHICKEN BREAST HALVES

2   TABLESPOONS FRESH THYME LEAVES

1/2 TEASPOON COARSE SEA SALT

6   PEPPERCORNS

3   TABLESPOONS SOFT GOAT CHEESE

1   CUP COARSELY CHOPPED BABY ARUGULA LEAVES

1   TEASPOON DRAINED SMALL CAPERS

Nutty, sweet baby arugula leaves, seasoned with capers and bound with goat cheese, make a savory stuffing to slip under the skin of chicken breasts. Young spinach leaves might be used instead of arugula. Roasted Yukon Gold potatoes, crushed with a fork and drizzled with olive oil, are the only accompaniment I need for this easy-to-make dish. If there are any leftovers, I slice the cold chicken and place it atop a salad of arugula and romaine.

Preheat the oven to 375 degrees F.

To make a pocket for the stuffing, loosen the skin on each chicken breast half by carefully slipping your fingers between the skin and the flesh. Do not detach the skin or tear any holes in it.

In a small spice grinder or coffee grinder, or using a mortar and pestle, grind together the thyme, salt, and peppercorns to a powder. Rub the chicken all over with the seasoning mixture and set aside.

In a small food processor or blender, combine the cheese and arugula and purée to make a paste. Transfer to a small bowl and stir in the capers. Using a small knife, spread some of the cheese mixture between the skin and flesh of each chicken breast half.

Place the chicken, skin-side up, on a baking sheet. Bake, basting once or twice with the pan juices, until the skin is golden brown and the juices run clear when a breast is pierced with the tip of a sharp knife, 35 to 40 minutes. Serve immediately.

mole verde chicken

1	CHICKEN, ABOUT 3 POUNDS, CUT INTO SERVING PIECES, OR 3 POUNDS CHICKEN THIGHS AND BREASTS
1	YELLOW ONION, HALF WHOLE, HALF COARSELY CHOPPED
1	TEASPOON FRESHLY GROUND PEPPER
1	1-INCH CUBE PEELED FRESH GINGER
1	TEASPOON SALT, PLUS MORE AS NEEDED
4	GREEN ANAHEIM CHILES
2	TO 4 SERRANO CHILES
3	CUPS WATER
4	TOMATILLOS
2	TABLESPOONS VEGETABLE OIL
1	TABLESPOON PUMPKIN SEEDS
2	TEASPOONS SESAME SEEDS
8	BLANCHED ALMONDS
2	CLOVES GARLIC, PEELED
1	GREEN BELL PEPPER, SEEDED, DERIBBED, AND COARSELY CHOPPED
1	TABLESPOON UNSALTED PEANUT BUTTER
2	ALLSPICE BERRIES
1	TOMATO, PEELED, SEEDED, AND CHOPPED

Moles are literally concoctions, and they include many ingredients, especially seeds, nuts, and various spices. The most well known is a very dark mole, which contains chocolate. Green mole, or mole verde, acquires its intense color from romaine lettuce, parsley, and fresh green Anaheim chiles. Pumpkin seeds, sesame seeds, and almonds help to thicken the sauce as well as flavor it. Served with steaming-hot corn tortillas and seasoned rice, this chicken dish makes a satisfying meal.

Put the chicken in a large pot and add water to cover by 2 inches. Add the 1/2 onion, pepper, ginger, and 1/2 teaspoon of the salt. Bring to a boil over high heat, reduce the heat to medium, and cook until the chicken is tender when pierced with a fork, 40 to 45 minutes. Using tongs, transfer the chicken to a colander to drain. When the chicken is cool enough to handle, remove the skin if desired. Skim the excess fat off the broth and reserve 3 cups of the broth.

Put the Anaheim and serrano chiles under a preheated broiler or over a direct flame on a gas stove and roast until the skin is charred, 3 to 4 minutes on each side, depending upon the heat.

Remove the stems and seeds and discard. Coarsely chop the chiles and put them in a blender or food processor. In a medium saucepan over medium heat, bring the water to a boil. Add the tomatillos, papery husks and all, and cook for 5 minutes. Drain. When the tomatillos are cool enough to handle, remove the papery husks and discard. Add the tomatillos and 1 cup of the reserved broth, and purée until smooth. Let stand for 15 to 20 minutes to allow the flavors to develop.

Preheat the oven to 350 degrees F.

In a small skillet over medium-high heat, heat the oil. Add the pumpkin seeds, sesame seeds, and almonds and sauté until the almonds are golden, 2 to 3 minutes. Add the seeds and nuts to the blender or food processor with the chile mixture. Add the garlic, chopped onion, bell pepper, peanut butter, allspice, and tomato and purée until smooth. Add about 1/2 cup of the reserved broth, the parsley, lettuce, and tortilla and purée. The mixture should be green and rather thick. If it is too thick, add a little more broth. You may not use all of the reserved broth, depending upon the water content of the vegetables.

1	CUP CHOPPED FRESH FLAT-LEAF PARSLEY
1	LARGE HEAD ROMAINE LETTUCE, LEAVES TORN INTO PIECES
1	CORN TORTILLA, TORN INTO SEVERAL PIECES

Put the mole in a medium saucepan over medium heat and cook, stirring from time to time, until it turns darker green, about 10 minutes. Add the remaining 1/2 teaspoon salt. Taste and add more salt if desired.

Put the chicken in a large ovenproof dish. Drizzle with 2 tablespoons of the reserved broth, cover, and bake until heated through, about 20 minutes. Transfer the chicken to a deep serving dish and ladle the hot mole sauce over it.

roast chicken with mâche, corn bread, and walnut stuffing   SERVES 4

corn bread

1¹/₂	CUPS ALL-PURPOSE FLOUR
¹/₄	CUP SUGAR
¹/₂	CUP CORNMEAL
1	TABLESPOON BAKING POWDER
¹/₂	TEASPOON SALT
1¹/₄	CUPS MILK
2	EGGS, BEATEN
¹/₃	CUP CORN OR OTHER VEGETABLE OIL
3	TABLESPOONS UNSALTED BUTTER, MELTED
2	GENEROUS TABLESPOONS CRUMBLED DRIED SAGE

roast chicken

1	CHICKEN, 3¹/₂ TO 4 POUNDS
1	TEASPOON SALT
1	TEASPOON FRESHLY GROUND PEPPER
2	TEASPOONS DRIED THYME
1	TEASPOON CRUMBLED DRIED SAGE
³/₄	CUP (ABOUT 6 OUNCES) WALNUTS
2	TABLESPOONS UNSALTED BUTTER
1	TABLESPOON MINCED YELLOW ONION
1	CLOVE GARLIC, MINCED
1	CUP CHICKEN BROTH
¹/₂	CUP DRY WHITE WINE
3	CUPS MÂCHE, PLUS MORE FOR GARNISHING

Imbued with both sweet and savory flavors, this light stuffing is dotted with clusters of mâche that gently steam during roasting. Toasted walnuts echo the nuttiness of the mâche, and the corn bread provides the perfect foil to a juicy, succulent chicken. The corn bread, fluffy and well seasoned with sage, can be made a day or two ahead. Finely chopped chard or kale might be substituted for the mâche.

To make the corn bread: Preheat the oven to 350 degrees F. Butter a 9-inch square baking dish.

In a large bowl, combine the flour, sugar, cornmeal, baking powder, and salt and stir together. In a medium bowl, combine the milk, eggs, oil, and melted butter and stir well. Pour the milk mixture into the flour mixture and stir just until everything is well moistened. Stir in the sage. Pour the batter into the prepared baking dish and bake until the corn bread is puffed and golden and pulls away slightly from the sides of the dish, 35 to 40 minutes. Transfer the pan to a wire rack and let cool.

If making the corn bread a day or two ahead, let cool completely, about 45 minutes, then cover with aluminum foil or plastic wrap and store at room temperature. The stuffing requires only half of the corn bread, so use the remainder for another dish or enjoy on its own.

Keep the oven set at 350 degrees F.

Remove the gizzard, heart, and liver from the chicken cavity and finely chop them. Set aside. Discard the neck or reserve for another use. Wash and dry the chicken inside and out and pat dry with paper towels. Rub the chicken inside and out with the salt, pepper, thyme, and sage. Set aside.

In a dry medium skillet over medium heat, toast the walnuts, stirring occasionally, until they are lightly golden and fragrant, 4 to 5 minutes. Remove from the heat, let cool, and chop coarsely. Set aside.

(continued on following page)

(continued)

In the same skillet over medium-high heat, melt the butter. When it foams, add the onion and sauté until shiny and nearly translucent, 2 to 3 minutes. Add the garlic, the chopped gizzard, heart, and liver, and sauté until the innards are no longer red, 2 to 3 minutes. Transfer to a large bowl. Return the skillet to medium-high heat and pour in the chicken broth and wine.

Bring to a boil and reduce to 1 cup, 4 to 5 minutes.

Break up half of the corn bread and add to the bowl with the onion mixture. Add the walnuts and the 3 cups mâche and stir to combine. Pour in the broth mixture and stir gently several times, leaving the corn bread chunky, not pasty.

Stuff about half of the corn bread mixture into the chicken cavity. Do not pack too tightly or too loosely; it's OK if a bit of stuffing peeks out of the cavity. Tie the legs together with kitchen string and put the chicken, breast-side up, in a medium roasting pan.

Lightly oil a small baking dish and put the remaining stuffing in it. Set aside. About 40 minutes before the chicken is done, cover the dish and bake until the stuffing is lightly browned on top, about 40 minutes.

Roast the chicken until it is golden brown and the juices of the deep inner thigh run clear when pierced with the tip of a sharp knife, about 1¼ hours. An instant-read thermometer inserted into the thickest part of the thigh, away from the bone, should register 175 degrees F. Transfer the chicken to a cutting board, cover loosely with aluminum foil, and let stand for 10 to 15 minutes before carving.

Scoop the stuffing from the cavity and transfer it to a large platter. Carve the chicken into serving pieces and arrange them on the platter. Garnish with the mâche. Serve the additional stuffing alongside.

pork tenderloin stuffed with chard and mushrooms

1 PORK TENDERLOIN, ABOUT 1½ POUNDS, BUTTERFLIED AND POUNDED TO ABOUT ¾-INCH THICKNESS

1½ TEASPOONS SALT

½ TEASPOON FRESHLY GROUND PEPPER

2 TABLESPOONS, PLUS 1 TEASPOON EXTRA-VIRGIN OLIVE OIL

1 SHALLOT, MINCED

2 OUNCES CLEANED AND ROUGHLY CHOPPED FRESH MOREL MUSHROOMS OR STEMMED SHIITAKE MUSHROOMS (ABOUT 1 CUP)

1 BUNCH CHARD

2 CUPS WATER

1 TABLESPOON UNSALTED BUTTER

1 CUP DRY WHITE WINE

When sliced, the stuffed tenderloin displays delicate rounds patterned with dark green spirals. I like to serve these with creamy polenta topped with a nubbin of Gorgonzola cheese, or Twice-Baked Potatoes with Escarole and Gruyère (page 136). Chard is used for the stuffing, but you can substitute spinach or kale. Precook the kale for 15 minutes rather than the 1 to 2 minutes recommended for the more tender chard or spinach.

Preheat the oven to 350 degrees F.

Rub the pork tenderloin on both sides with 1/2 teaspoon of the salt and 1/4 teaspoon of the pepper. Lay the tenderloin out flat, butterflied-side up, and set aside.

In a large ovenproof skillet over medium heat, heat the 2 tablespoons olive oil. Add the shallot and sauté until translucent, 3 to 4 minutes. Add the mushrooms, 1/2 teaspoon of the salt, and the remaining 1/4 teaspoon pepper. Sauté until the mushrooms are soft and release their juices, about 5 minutes. Transfer the mushrooms to a medium bowl. Set the skillet over high heat, stirring until any juices are evaporated. Do not clean the skillet.

Using a sharp knife, cut along the edges of the wide midrib of the chard leaves and remove them. Discard the ribs. In a saucepan over high heat, bring the water to a boil and add the remaining 1/2 teaspoon salt. Add the chard and cook for 1 to 2 minutes. Drain in a colander. When the chard is cool enough to handle, finely chop it and squeeze out the excess liquid. Add the chard to the bowl with the mushrooms and stir to combine. Spread the mixture lengthwise along two thirds of the tenderloin in an even layer. Working from the edge with the filling, roll the tenderloin toward the unfilled side. Using 6 six-inch pieces of kitchen string, tie the rolled tenderloin at 2-inch intervals.

Set the skillet over medium-high heat and melt the butter with the 1 teaspoon olive oil. When the butter foams, add the tenderloin and brown on all sides, about 5 minutes total. Pour in the wine and cook for 1 minute, stirring to scrape up any bits that cling to the bottom of the pan. Transfer the skillet to the oven. Roast until the pork is firm to the touch and the juices run clear when the pork is pierced with the tip of a sharp knife, about 40 minutes. The internal temperature should be 150 degrees F. Transfer the pork to a cutting board and cover loosely with aluminum foil. Let stand for about 5 minutes, then cut crosswise into 1/2-inch-thick rounds. Arrange the rounds on a platter, drizzle with any pan juices, and serve immediately.

juniper-brined pork chops smothered with braised kale

2   QUARTS COLD WATER

1/2 CUP, PLUS 1/4 TEASPOON KOSHER SALT

10 JUNIPER BERRIES, LIGHTLY CRUSHED
    WITH THE BACK OF A KNIFE

4   PORK CHOPS, EACH ABOUT 1 INCH THICK

2   TABLESPOONS EXTRA-VIRGIN OLIVE OIL

1   LARGE BUNCH KALE

1   SMALL SHALLOT, FINELY CHOPPED

1/2 CUP CHICKEN BROTH

1/4 TEASPOON FRESHLY GROUND PEPPER

Brining the pork chops helps to keep them moist and flavors them with the woodsy sharpness of juniper, which is balanced by the robust taste of the braised kale. You can substitute cabbage, chard, or spinach, reducing the cooking time to 10 to 12 minutes for chard and 2 to 3 minutes for spinach so that the greens are just tender.

In a large nonreactive container, combine the water and the 1/2 cup salt and stir until the salt is dissolved, about 5 minutes. Add the juniper berries and pork chops. Refrigerate the chops, turning them once or twice, for 4 to 6 hours.

Preheat the oven to 350 degrees F.

Remove the chops and juniper berries from the brine and pat the chops dry. In an ovenproof skillet large enough to hold the chops in a single layer, heat 1 tablespoon of the olive oil over medium-high heat. Add the chops and brown them, about 2 minutes on each side. Add the juniper berries to the skillet and transfer to the oven. Roast until the meat is opaque in the center, about 35 minutes. Discard the juniper berries.

Meanwhile, using a sharp knife, cut the stems off the kale and discard. Coarsely chop the leaves. In a large skillet over medium heat, heat the remaining 1 tablespoon olive oil. Add the shallot and sauté until translucent, 2 to 3 minutes, then stir in the kale, chicken broth, the 1/4 teaspoon salt, and the pepper. Reduce the heat to low, cover, and cook until the kale is tender enough to cut with a fork, about 15 minutes. Serve the pork chops smothered with the kale.

stuffed cabbage leaves, italian style

sauce

2	TABLESPOONS EXTRA-VIRGIN OLIVE OIL
2	TABLESPOONS MINCED YELLOW ONION
2	CLOVES GARLIC, MINCED
1	CAN (14 OUNCES) ITALIAN PLUM TOMATOES, CHOPPED, WITH JUICES
1/2	TEASPOON SALT
1/2	TEASPOON FRESHLY GROUND PEPPER
1	BAY LEAF
1/2	TEASPOON DRIED OREGANO

3 OR 4 FRESH THYME SPRIGS, OR 1/2 TEASPOON DRIED THYME

This recipe comes from my neighbor in Provence, who is originally from Calabria, on the toe of Italy. The dish is filled with the aromas of garlic, parsley, and spicy meat that I associate with her kitchen. She and her husband tend a huge garden, and they always grow plenty of cabbages of all different kinds. Sometimes she uses Savoy cabbage for this dish and other times, flat-headed or round ones, but the light tomato sauce is always the same. It just covers the wrapped packets so they stay moist but aren't smothered. The sauce can be made one day ahead and refrigerated.

To make the sauce: In a large saucepan over medium-high heat, heat the olive oil. Add the onion and sauté until nearly translucent, 3 to 4 minutes. Add the garlic and sauté for 1 minute, then add the tomatoes and their juices. Stir and add the salt, pepper, bay leaf, oregano, and thyme. Reduce the heat to low and simmer, stirring occasionally, until the sauce is thickened, about 20 minutes.

Meanwhile, make the stuffed cabbage: Put the bread in a large bowl and pour the milk over it. Set aside.

In a large pot over high heat, bring the water to a boil. Add 1 teaspoon of the salt. Cutting at the base of the cabbage, remove 8 large yet tender outer leaves. Cut the remaining cabbage in half, cut out the solid core, and discard it. Coarsely chop the inner leaves.

Put the whole leaves in the boiling water and cook until they are soft and shiny, about 1 minute. Using tongs, transfer the leaves to a colander, run cold water over them, and set aside. Put the coarsely chopped inner leaves in the boiling water and cook for about 1 minute. Drain in a colander and run cold water over them. Transfer the inner leaves to a cutting board, finely chop enough to make 2 cups, and squeeze them dry. Reserve any remaining leaves.

Preheat the oven to 350 degrees F. Grease a baking dish with olive oil.

Squeeze the bread dry, discarding any excess milk, and return the bread to the bowl. Add the 2 cups finely chopped cabbage, the onion, garlic, 1/2 teaspoon of the salt, the pepper, parsley,

stuffed cabbage

2   CUPS TORN STALE BREAD, PREFERABLY STURDY
    COUNTRY BREAD OR A BAGUETTE

1/2 CUP MILK

2   QUARTS WATER

1 1/2 TO 2 TEASPOONS SALT

1   HEAD GREEN CABBAGE, ABOUT 1 POUND

3   TABLESPOONS MINCED YELLOW ONION

2   CLOVES GARLIC, MINCED

1 1/2 TEASPOONS FRESHLY GROUND PEPPER

1/4 CUP CHOPPED FRESH FLAT-LEAF PARSLEY

1/2 TEASPOON DRIED THYME

1/2 TEASPOON DRIED OREGANO

1   POUND BULK ITALIAN SAUSAGE, SPICY OR MILD

thyme, oregano, and sausage. Using your hands, mix well. The filling should easily hold together in a somewhat sticky mass. Add more salt if desired.

Lay a cabbage leaf, cupped-side up, in your hand. Put 2 generous tablespoons of the filling in the lower-middle part of the leaf. Fold the thick rib end over the filling, then fold over each side, envelope-style. Finally, fold over the top. Place the cabbage roll, seam-side down, in the prepared baking dish. Repeat with the remaining leaves. Sprinkle with a few of the remaining coarsely chopped leaves.

Spoon the sauce over the cabbage rolls and bake until the sauce is bubbling around the edges, the rolls are firm to the touch, and the cabbage is easily pierced with a fork, about 35 minutes. Remove the bay leaf and discard. Using a spatula, remove the cabbage rolls and serve.

NOT SURPRISINGLY, GREENS ARE JUST AS VERSATILE IN SIDE DISHES AS THEY ARE IN OTHER COURSES. STURDY GREENS, SUCH AS CABBAGE, ESCAROLE, AND BOK CHOY, CAN BE GRILLED, BRAISED, SAUTÉED, STIR-FRIED, OR EVEN STEAMED AND SERVED AS AN ACCOMPANIMENT FOR VIRTUALLY ANY MAIN COURSE.

When braising greens, you can create dozens of variations by using different liquids, such as white or red wine, or chicken or beef broth. You can also create variations for braising, sautéing, or stir-frying by adding seasonings like garlic, chives, coriander, cumin, or ginger. Sturdy greens combine beautifully with other vegetables, including sweet or hot peppers, mushrooms, beans, squash, or potatoes, making for near-endless options. Delicate greens—mâche, spinach, and arugula—are best quickly wilted in butter or broth for no more than a few minutes, then lightly seasoned and served.

OPPOSITE PAGE: Stir-fried Napa Cabbage, Bok Choy, and Hot Chiles (page 129)

creamed spinach gratin

3   POUNDS SPINACH, STEMMED

3   TABLESPOONS UNSALTED BUTTER

2 1/2 TABLESPOONS ALL-PURPOSE FLOUR

1   CUP MILK

1/4   TEASPOON SALT

1/4   TEASPOON FRESHLY GROUND PEPPER

1/4   TEASPOON FRESHLY GRATED NUTMEG

1/2   CUP FRESH BREAD CRUMBS

1/4   CUP FRESHLY GRATED PARMESAN CHEESE
     (OPTIONAL)

I love the velvety richness of creamed spinach with a crunchy topping, and I make it year-round. In summer, I spoon the spinach and sauce into a buttered gratin dish and add a layer of sliced vine-ripened tomatoes plus a sprinkling of thyme, salt, pepper, and bread crumbs. Then I serve the hot gratin with a roasted leg of lamb seasoned with herbes de Provence, or with thick grilled steaks and baked potatoes. This creamy dish can also be prepared with chard or kale, cooking them in boiling water for about 15 minutes.

Preheat the oven to 450 degrees F.

Bring a large pot of water to a boil over high heat. Add the spinach and cook until it is limp but still bright green, 2 to 5 minutes, depending upon the tenderness of the leaves. Drain in a colander and rinse with cold running water to stop the cooking and preserve the color. Using you hands, squeeze out the excess liquid, then chop the spinach finely or coarsely, depending upon your preference. Set aside.

In a medium saucepan over medium-high heat, melt 1 1/2 tablespoons of the butter. When it foams, remove the pan from the heat and whisk in the flour to make a roux, or paste. Return the pan to medium-high heat and pour in the milk a little at a time, whisking to prevent lumps from forming. When all the milk has been incorporated, whisk in the salt, pepper, and nutmeg. Reduce the heat to low and simmer until the taste of flour has dissipated and the sauce has thickened, about 15 minutes. If the sauce seems too thin, increase the heat to medium-high and cook until it is medium-thick, 2 to 3 minutes longer. Remove from the heat.

Heavily butter a medium gratin or baking dish, then put in the chopped spinach. Pour the béchamel sauce over it and, using a fork, lift the spinach a little so the sauce runs through it. In a small saucepan over medium heat, melt the remaining 1 1/2 tablespoons butter. Scatter the bread crumbs over the spinach and pour the butter over the crumbs. Scatter the cheese over the top if desired. Bake until the top is golden and the sauce is bubbling around the edges, about 10 minutes. Serve immediately.

balsamic-braised radicchio

3   TABLESPOONS EXTRA-VIRGIN OLIVE OIL

1   HEAD RADICCHIO, CORED AND LEAVES
    COARSELY CHOPPED

¼   TEASPOON SALT

¼   TEASPOON FRESHLY GROUND PEPPER

2   TABLESPOONS BALSAMIC VINEGAR

With its sturdy leaves and pleasant bitter undertones, radicchio stands up especially well to high heat and big flavors, like the balsamic vinegar used here. I like to serve this dish with hearty fare, such as venison steaks, duck, and well-seasoned squab or quail, accompanied by polenta or risotto. Escarole and Belgian endive can be prepared in this way as well.

In a medium skillet or sauté pan over medium-high heat, heat the olive oil. Add the radicchio and sauté, stirring it often, until it begins to brown, 3 to 4 minutes. Stir in the salt, pepper, and vinegar. Reduce the heat to low, cover, and cook, stirring once or twice, until most of the liquid is absorbed, 5 to 7 minutes. Serve immediately.

belgian endive braised in white wine and herbs

8   HEADS BELGIAN ENDIVE

1/2   TEASPOON SALT

1/4   TEASPOON FRESHLY GROUND PEPPER

3   FRESH THYME SPRIGS

4   FRESH FLAT-LEAF PARSLEY SPRIGS

4   TABLESPOONS UNSALTED BUTTER

1/3   CUP DRY WHITE WINE

Belgian endive is a vegetable frequently served as a side dish in European restaurants and homes, especially in northern France, Holland, and Belgium. Often it is simply braised in butter along with a little chicken or other broth, wine, cider, or beer and perhaps some aromatics. After the endive is braised, it is slipped under the broiler, where it turns a rich golden brown. Serve this soothing dish alongside meat or poultry. Wedges of cabbage can be cooked in a similar fashion.

Cut a round of parchment paper to fit inside a medium skillet or sauté pan with a tight-fitting lid. Heavily butter the pan.

Using a small, sharp knife, cut an inverted V in the base of each Belgian endive to remove the core. Tuck the endive snugly in a single layer in the prepared pan. Sprinkle with the salt and pepper, tuck the thyme and parsley among the endive, and dot with 3 tablespoons of the butter. Set the pan over medium-high heat and, when the butter begins to melt, slowly pour in the wine. Cook until the wine is reduced by half, 3 to 4 minutes, then reduce the heat to low.

Using 1 teaspoon of the butter, grease one side of the parchment round. Lay the parchment, buttered-side down, on top of the endive, gently pressing it in place. Cover with the lid and cook until the endive is soft and tender and turning a faint gold, 35 to 40 minutes. Check from time to time that there is still liquid in the pan, and add a little water if necessary.

Preheat the broiler.

When the endive is ready, uncover the pan and remove and discard the parchment and the herbs. Boil off any remaining liquid. Dot the endive with the remaining 2 teaspoons butter and broil just until the endive is golden brown, 2 to 3 minutes. Serve immediately.

braising greens with lemon and garlic

2 POUNDS MIXED YOUNG, TENDER GREENS CHOSEN FROM THE FOLLOWING LIST (OR USE A PREPARED BRAISING MIX):
- ORNAMENTAL CABBAGE
- ORNAMENTAL KALE
- RED RUSSIAN KALE
- LACINATO KALE
- BLUE KALE
- RED CHARD
- GREEN CHARD
- GOLDEN CHARD
- MESCAROLE
- FRISÉE
- SPINACH
- RADICCHIO

1½ TABLESPOONS EXTRA-VIRGIN OLIVE OIL

1 CLOVE GARLIC, GRATED OR MINCED

½ TEASPOON SALT

JUICE OF 1 LEMON

A mixture of young greens, such as different varieties of kale, chard, escarole, frisée, spinach, and radicchio, are all good for braising. I think a mixture provides an intriguing contrast in flavors and colors, especially when flowering kales, red and golden chard, and red radicchio are included, although any single green can be cooked in the same fashion. Or try using a prepared braising mix, available in some produce markets. More mature greens can be cooked this way as well, but it is best to remove the coarse midribs and to increase the cooking time by about 15 minutes, or until the greens are tender. Braised greens complement rich meat dishes beautifully. I like to serve them alongside roast pork or lamb, braised lamb or veal shanks, and barbecued ribs.

Separate the leaves from the heads if necessary and put them in a large bowl of cold water. Heat a large skillet or sauté pan over medium heat and put the greens, undried and dripping with water, in the pan. Reduce the heat to medium-low, cover, and cook for about 2 minutes. Uncover the pan. The greens should be wilting and there should be liquid in the pan. If not, add 1/2 cup water. Cover and continue to cook until the greens are thoroughly wilted but still bright green and colorful, about 6 minutes.

Pour off any liquid and add the olive oil, garlic, and salt. Increase the heat to medium-high, stirring to coat the greens with the oil, and cook off excess liquid, 1 to 2 minutes. Add the lemon juice, which will sizzle, then transfer the greens to a serving dish. Serve immediately, piping hot.

stir-fried napa cabbage, bok choy, and hot chiles

¼   CUP CORN OR OTHER LIGHT VEGETABLE OIL

2   TO 4 SMALL DRIED RED CHILES, SUCH AS JAPONES
    OR BIRD'S EYE, SEEDED, OR 1 TEASPOON
    RED PEPPER FLAKES

2   CLOVES GARLIC, MINCED

1   LARGE BOK CHOY OR 4 GREEN-STEMMED BOK CHOY,
    COARSELY CHOPPED

½   HEAD NAPA CABBAGE, SHREDDED (4 TO 5 CUPS)

1   TABLESPOON FERMENTED BLACK BEANS

1   TEASPOON LIGHT SOY SAUCE

The mild flavor of napa cabbage and the slightly sharper taste of bok choy join together to make a simple accompaniment for meat and poultry. I like to serve this stir-fry with grilled pork and shrimp kabobs along with rice or noodles. For an extra fillip, sprinkle the greens with toasted sesame seeds. Fermented black beans are a common Chinese seasoning and may be found in the Asian ingredient sections of most supermarkets. Any cabbage can be used in this dish, and chard is good as well.

In a wok or deep skillet over high heat, heat the oil. Add the chiles and garlic and stir until fragrant, about 30 seconds. Add the bok choy and sauté, stirring, until the pieces of stalk are soft and tender but still hold their shape, about 4 minutes. Add the cabbage, and sauté, stirring until it is limp and just turning a bit golden, 3 to 4 minutes. Stir in the black beans and soy sauce and cook for 1 minute. Serve immediately.

sweet-and-sour red cabbage

1	HEAD RED CABBAGE, 1½ TO 2 POUNDS
2	BACON SLICES, CHOPPED
3	TABLESPOONS UNSALTED BUTTER
¼	YELLOW ONION, MINCED
2	APPLES (ANY KIND), PEELED, CORED, AND GRATED
2	CUPS RED WINE VINEGAR
1	TABLESPOON PEELED AND GRATED FRESH GINGER (OPTIONAL)
1¼	TEASPOONS SALT
½	TEASPOON FRESHLY GROUND PEPPER
2½	TABLESPOONS HONEY

Since this is one of my very favorite dishes, I grow plenty of red cabbages in my garden so I can make it whenever the mood strikes. After long, slow cooking, the cabbage emerges tender and soft rose in color, glistening with the sweet-and-sour braising liquids. I serve it with pork, game, and sausages of all kinds. For a simple garnish, dice 1 small apple and sauté for 2 minutes in 2 to 3 tablespoons of butter.

Using a sharp knife, quarter the cabbage lengthwise, cut out the solid core, and discard it. Cut the quarters lengthwise into very thin slices. Put the cabbage in a large bowl or pot of cold water and set aside.

In a heavy-bottomed saucepan or Dutch oven over low heat, fry the bacon until it has rendered its fat and is crisp and brown, about 6 minutes. Using a slotted spoon, remove the bacon and reserve for another use. Reserve the fat in the pan. Increase the heat to medium and add the butter. When it foams, add the onion and sauté until translucent, about 3 minutes. Remove the cabbage from the water and, without drying it, add it to the pan.

It might seem impossible to fit it in the pan, but the cabbage will cook down considerably. Cover, reduce the heat to low, and simmer until the cabbage is reduced by one fourth and is almost pink in color, about 10 minutes.

Add the apples, vinegar, ginger if desired, and 1 teaspoon of the salt. Cover and cook until the cabbage is reduced by half and the apples have nearly dissolved, about 50 minutes.

Stir in the pepper, the remaining ¼ teaspoon salt, and the honey. Cover and cook until the cabbage is slightly darker and quite shiny and the flavors are blending, about 40 minutes. Uncover, increase the heat to high, and boil off any excess liquid. The cabbage should be moist and supple but not swimming in liquid. Serve hot, warm, or at room temperature.

baby peas steamed with butter and mâche

3   TABLESPOONS UNSALTED BUTTER

2   TABLESPOONS MINCED SHALLOT

1½ POUNDS FRESH PEAS IN THE POD,
    SHELLED (ABOUT 1½ CUPS)

¼   CUP WATER, PLUS MORE AS NEEDED

½   TEASPOON SALT

¼   TEASPOON FRESHLY GROUND WHITE PEPPER

1   CUP MÂCHE

This recipe is inspired by a classic French dish in which tender young peas are slowly braised in butter with bundles of butterhead lettuce. Here, the mâche, which wilts quickly, is added at the last minute, lending its bright green color and contrasting flavor to the peas. This dish is best prepared with the most tender peas, as it is quite delicate. As an alternative, use the traditional butterhead lettuce, quartered and tied with kitchen string into bundles.

In a saucepan over medium-high heat, melt the butter. When it foams, add the shallot, cover, and reduce the heat to very low. Cook the shallot until it is very soft but not browned, about 5 minutes. Add the peas, the ¼ cup water, the salt, and white pepper. Cover, increase the heat to low, and simmer until the peas are tender, about 10 minutes. If necessary, add more water during cooking.

Using kitchen shears, cut the mâche sprigs in half.

When the peas are tender, layer the mâche over the peas. Cover and cook for 1 minute, then remove from the heat and serve immediately.

lentils and carrots with kale

1   BUNCH KALE

3   CUPS WATER

1   CUP FRENCH GREEN LENTILS

2   CLOVES GARLIC, MINCED

1   MEDIUM CARROT, PEELED AND FINELY DICED

1/2 TEASPOON SALT

1/4 TEASPOON FRESHLY GROUND PEPPER

Kale adds a deep, complex flavor to the traditional duo of lentils and carrots. A few spoonfuls are the perfect foil for grilled or roasted pork chops, roast beef, or lamb. The earthiness of this dish counterbalances the richness of the meats. Chard or cabbage could be used instead of the kale.

Using a sharp knife, cut the stems off the kale and discard. Cut the leaves crosswise into thin strips and set aside.

In a medium saucepan over high heat, bring the water to a boil. Add the lentils, garlic, carrot, salt, and pepper. Reduce the heat to low and cook until the lentils are tender, 30 to 40 minutes. Put the kale on top of the lentils, cover, and cook until the kale is wilted and tender, 5 to 7 minutes. Remove from the heat and stir the kale into the lentils. Using a slotted spoon, transfer to a serving dish, leaving the excess liquid in the pan.

butternut squash with arugula

1   BUTTERNUT SQUASH, ABOUT 2 POUNDS

2   TEASPOONS UNSALTED BUTTER

1/4   TEASPOON SALT

1/4   TEASPOON FRESHLY GROUND PEPPER

1/4   TEASPOON DRIED THYME

2   TABLESPOONS CHICKEN BROTH

2   CUPS BABY ARUGULA LEAVES

1   TEASPOON FINELY CHOPPED TOASTED PECANS
    (OPTIONAL)

With its deep, earthy, flavors, slow-roasted squash atop a bed of wilted arugula makes a comforting side dish to serve with assertively seasoned game and beef. Spinach can be used as well.

Preheat the oven to 350 degrees F.

Cut the squash in half lengthwise. Using a metal spoon, scoop out the seeds and fibers. Put the squash halves, cut-side up, on a baking sheet or in a baking dish. Dot the tops with the butter and sprinkle with the salt, pepper, and thyme. Roast until very soft and tender, about 13/4 hours. When the squash is cool enough to handle, scoop out the flesh into a medium bowl. Using a fork, mash it coarsely, just enough to distribute the seasonings.

In a medium skillet over medium-high heat, bring the broth to simmer. Add the arugula 1 cup at a time and cook until it just wilts, about 30 seconds. Using a slotted spoon, transfer to a bowl. To serve, divide the arugula among 4 plates or bowls, top with a scoop of the squash, and sprinkle with the pecans if desired.

twice-baked potatoes with escarole and gruyère

2   MEDIUM RUSSET POTATOES

1/2 TABLESPOON EXTRA-VIRGIN OLIVE OIL

2   TABLESPOONS UNSALTED BUTTER

1/2 HEAD ESCAROLE, PREFERABLY PALE
    INNER LEAVES ONLY

1/4 CUP CHICKEN BROTH

2   OUNCES GRUYÈRE CHEESE, CUT INTO SMALL CUBES,
    PLUS 1 TABLESPOON FRESHLY GRATED CHEESE

1/2 TEASPOON COARSE SEA SALT

1/2 TEASPOON FRESHLY GROUND PEPPER

Braised in butter and chicken broth, escarole lends a slightly sweet bitterness to the potatoes, which are exceptionally creamy because of the addition of Gruyère cheese. Rubbing the potatoes with olive oil before baking produces firm, crisp skins, which nicely support the filling, and sea salt provides little bursts of flavor. I serve these potatoes to accompany dishes as diverse as roast chicken, barbecued ribs, and baked fish. Radicchio or frisée might be substituted for the escarole.

Preheat the oven to 350 degrees F.

Rub the potatoes all over with the olive oil and put them on a rack in the oven. Bake until the skin is shiny and is starting to crisp and wrinkle slightly, about 1¹/2 hours.

Meanwhile, in a medium skillet over medium-high heat, melt the butter. When it foams, add the escarole, cover, and reduce the heat to low. Let the escarole sweat until it wilts and has released its juices but has not yet started to brown, 6 to 7 minutes. Add the chicken broth, cover, and cook until nearly all of the liquid has evaporated and the escarole is meltingly soft,

about 3 minutes. Transfer the escarole to a cutting board and finely chop. Set aside.

Remove the potatoes from the oven; keep the oven set at 350 degrees F. Grease a medium baking dish with olive oil.

Cut the potatoes in half lengthwise. Using a metal spoon, scoop out the flesh to within about 1/4 inch of the skin and put in a medium bowl. Add the cheese cubes and, using a potato masher or a fork, mash and stir them into the potatoes until they melt, 1 to 2 minutes. Stir in the escarole, salt, and pepper. Fill each potato half with an equal amount of the mixture, mounding it slightly. Top with a sprinkling of the grated cheese.

Put the potatoes in the prepared baking dish. Bake until the cheese melts and is just beginning to brown and the potato skins are crisp, about 30 minutes. Serve immediately.

index

LIQUID/DRY MEASURES

U.S.		METRIC
1/4	TEASPOON	1.25 MILLILITERS
1/2	TEASPOON	2.5 MILLILITERS
1	TEASPOON	5 MILLILITERS
1	TABLESPOON (3 teaspoons)	15 MILLILITERS
1	FLUID OUNCE (2 tablespoons)	30 MILLILITERS
1/4	CUP	60 MILLILITERS
1/3	CUP	80 MILLILITERS
1/2	CUP	120 MILLILITERS
1	CUP	240 MILLILITERS
1	PINT (2 cups)	480 MILLILITERS
1	QUART (4 cups, 32 ounces)	960 MILLILITERS
1	GALLON (4 QUARTS)	3.84 LITERS
1	OUNCE (by weight)	28 GRAMS
1	POUND	454 GRAMS
2.2	POUNDS	1 KILOGRAM

LENGTH

U.S.	METRIC
1/8 INCH	3 MILLIMETERS
1/4 INCH	6 MILLIMETERS
1/2 INCH	12 MILLIMETERS
1 INCH	2.5 CENTIMETERS

OVEN TEMPERATURE

FAHRENHEIT	CELSIUS	GAS
250	120	1/2
275	140	1
300	150	2
325	160	3
350	180	4
375	190	5
400	200	6
425	220	7
450	230	8
475	240	9
500	260	10